THE SYNERGETIC FOLLOWER:

Changing Our World Without Being the Leader

The Synergetic Follower: Changing our world without being the leader.

Copyright © 2011 by Kurt Madden

First Edition: August 2011

Library of Congress Cataloging-in-Publication Data is available upon request.

ISBN-13: 978-1463684440

ISBN-10: 1463684444

10   9   8   7   6   5   4   3   2   1

Book designed by Kris Madden

Printed in the United States of America

This book is dedicated to the many followers who seek to make the world a better place, but would prefer to accomplish it without being the leader.

I would also like to thank my family and friends who encouraged me to stay focused and finish this book amidst all the wonderful distractions of life.

Contents

Preface

For the last decade, I have been intrigued with the impact followers can have on corporations, businesses and organizations. In researching this group it became clear that a specific type of follower was significantly impacting and transforming their business, their organization and the world around them.

I call this follower: "The Synergetic Follower." They are content not to be the leader of their organization and are not interested in climbing the corporate ladder. Instead they are focused on working together with their colleagues in creative, innovative and productive ways to move the mission of their organization forward.

Over the past forty years of being the employee or the employer, I have found myself in almost every position from a front-line-follower (dishwasher) to a follower-leader to a leader's-leader to, occasionally, the CEO/President. In addition, my volunteer work with many nonprofits and community boards ranged from event organizer to amateur brick layer to Board Chair.

I have thoroughly enjoyed every position I've held—well, maybe not the dishwasher one so much. I eagerly took advantage of the opportunities to learn, fail, succeed, grow and work with others toward a shared goal. The following pages reflect what I have learned, regardless of whether I was in a follower or leader position or both (which is where I find myself most of the time).

My hope is that this book will encourage you to think differently about what it means to be a follower—and realize the transforming impact you can have as a Synergetic Follower.

Introduction
The Synergetic Follower

Why the term, "The Synergetic Follower?" Synergetic, is defined as, "working together in a creative, innovative, and productive manner."[1] We'll see that it's a term for followers who want to change the world without having to be the top leader.

There are thousands of books, millions of articles, and a bazillion blogs and tweets on leadership. There are also books and articles on followership, but many of them are from the viewpoint of the leader, that is, how to recruit and develop good followers. However, there are a few good books on being a follower, especially *Courageous Follower*,[2] about standing up to leadership and *The Art of Followership*.[3]

Let's mention a couple of things this book is not about. This is not about followers overthrowing leaders. That's a lot of work and if we overthrow the leader we just have to put someone else in charge. It's also not about being a servant or groupie to our leader—kissing the ring every day is not our idea of success. We're also not going to talk about how to make lots of cash being a Synergetic Follower, we'll leave that to late-night TV infomercials. Finally, this is not about being a follower on Twitter or being a friend on Facebook. Both activities can produce success, but that's not what we mean by being a Synergetic Follower.

So who wants to be a follower? How many times has that question been asked? Not very often. As kids, we were always asked what we wanted to be when we grew up: teacher, policeman, doctor, astronaut or president. No one asked if we wanted to be office manager, help desk specialist, ambulance driver, space shuttle designer, or assistant to the president.

Instead we are encouraged to be the leader. We are told that being a follower is just the path we must trudge on to become a leader. As we move up the follower ranks, we will get to practice being a junior leader and that someday if we are patient, we will finally be "The Leader." We'll get the top job with all that comes with it, big pay, celebrity, fancy car, a huge house where we can host parties with fascinating people and of course have lots of followers who will be at our beck and call. It's the end game—it is what we're all supposed to be shooting for.

Of course, they neglect to tell us that often the pay for the top job barely covers the fancy car, the huge house, and the cost for the ex-spouses that were left behind on the climb to the top and that the people at the parties aren't all that fascinating and that followers don't always like following. They also don't tell us that when the top leader fails, the mistakes show up on the front page of the newspaper for all to see (sometimes accompanied with an unappealing photo or semi-funny cartoon caricature), that the money and followers disappear rapidly, celebrity turns to ridicule, and that no one wants to hire them because they obviously want to be in charge and wouldn't know how to follow.

This book is for those that aren't focused and driven to be The Leader. It's for those who want to make a difference, but don't need to be the top dog. There are lots of followers who make significant contributions to our businesses, organizations, and communities and are not trying to climb the ladder to be the leader. We'll look at what it takes to be a specific type of follower—a Synergetic Follower.

Chapter 1
The Power of Choice

In order to define what a Synergetic Follower is, we should begin with the most powerful and defining concept of followership. **As followers, we have an incredible power— it's the power of choosing who we want to follow and invest in.** Don't be underwhelmed by this statement. The significance of this choice of who to follow is often overlooked or disregarded. Let the idea sink in a little bit, maybe say it out loud once or twice (but not while your leader is nearby). In our leadership-focused world, where some successful leaders have the celebrity and income of rock stars and sports stars, the value of the followers behind the leader is often lost. This is not just one of the many concepts in followership—it is the absolute foundation of followership and the starting point for anyone who wants to be a Synergetic Follower.

As followers, why does this concept of choosing the leader get lost so often? It likely goes back to our first job. We didn't have experience or knowledge or skills, but we needed money and would work for almost anyone (even our parents) who gave us a chance. Over time, as we gained experience, knowledge and skills, we worked hard, we succeeded, we failed, we looked for better jobs that would pay us more and allow us to learn more in the areas we enjoyed. However, as we began our career, it seemed like we were always at the mercy of the potential employer. We were the ones offering ourselves— they were the ones who made the choices.

Now that we've moved past that first job (and maybe too many to count since then), we have something to offer a leader or organization. It's time to flip that old paradigm from our first job over on its head. We are now followers who provide knowledge, experience and skills, we're not kids anymore hoping for our first job. **We have a choice to stay and continue to contribute to our organization's success or leave and contribute to the success of someone else.** After all, our employer has the choice to keep us or let us go. We have a similar choice to follow our current leader or choose someone else.

While many tend to overlook the value of a follower, the best leaders understand that followers have a choice and that they can leave whenever they want to. Excellent leaders know that without good followers, they won't be successful. In reality, we evaluate our leaders by the success of the work done by their followers. We also look at the quality and quantity of their followers. Wall Street and venture capital analysts never look at just the leader before they invest in a company—they also look at the followers. Does the company have a sharp financial person? Do they have a creative designer that has a track record? Do they have someone who knows how to implement and get a product out the door? The follower behind the leader can sometimes be more important than the leader.

For example, drug companies work hard to recruit the best scientists and researchers. Chloroquine, one of the drugs that helped in the fight against malaria was discovered by a chemist, Hans Andersag, at Bayer laboratories in Germany in 1934.[4] In 1957, British virologist Alick Isaacs and the Swiss researcher Jean Lindenmann, at the National Institute for Medical Research in London discovered one of the most effective anti-cancer drugs, Interferon, Type I.[5] These individuals were staff researchers who worked for large companies or organizations—they weren't anywhere near the top of the organization, yet they saved millions of lives and changed their world.

If we take the time to look at who is following a leader, we can often predict their success or failure. This is often more visible in sports than in business, but the rules still apply. Think for just a moment about a sports team that we love. How do we feel when they recruit a player for a key position who is over-rated? We realize with that bad selection our hope for a season championship has been lost. The worst trade in baseball history? Some point to the "Midnight Massacre" when the New York Mets traded pitcher Tom Seaver to the Cincinnati Reds for Pat Zachry, Doug Flynn, Steve Henderson, and Dan Norman. Zachry had one good year, the rest were a bust along with the Mets. But Seaver continued his success with the Reds for many more seasons and entered the Baseball Hall of Fame.

They don't usually televise "personnel trades" in the business world (although Donald Trump's Apprentice may come close), but recruiting and hiring are constantly going on. Just as a good follower can change the whole company or organization, a bad one can hold a company back or ruin it. There are many leaders who selected or attracted the wrong followers and as a result never achieved the success they could have had. Successful leaders know this and they spend a considerable amount of time, effort and resources to recruit and retain outstanding followers.

As far back as the times of Niccolò Machiavelli this concept was understood. Machiavelli said, "The first method for estimating the intelligence of a ruler is to look at the men he has around him."[6] Machiavelli lived during the early 1500's, so this notion that leaders are judged by their followers has been around for a long time. It's easy to spot less-than-intelligent and unsuccessful leaders who prefer to surround themselves with sycophants and unskilled, inexperienced and sometimes unscrupulous followers. **But outstanding leaders know that they cannot be successful without recruiting and convincing good followers to make a choice to follow them.**

Some are saying, "I don't have a choice of who to work for!" So for a moment let's look at those followers who say, due to life's circumstances, that they do not have the ability to choose who they follow or work for. While there may be some who feel trapped in a work situation and unable to escape—they still have a choice. No one can force an individual to follow or work for them, although leaders sometimes treat followers as if they don't have a choice. If we look outside the developed countries, a peasant in a nation run by an evil dictator still has a choice to follow or not. Even, if in that nation, choosing not to follow could lead to imprisonment or worse. We agree that it may be tough to leave an evil dictator (and a detriment to our health), but people try to leave all the time. Our freedom to choose is powerful, but that doesn't make it easy. Usually the easy choice is to stay right where we are, but that doesn't always make it the best choice.

Let's reflect on that statement one more time: **No one can force us to follow or work for them.** We realize that the negative consequences that face us if we leave our job might make us "feel" like we have no choice, but the reality is that we could leave tomorrow, it happens every day. Let's also not forget that employment is not guaranteed. There are people who continue to stay even when they have the opportunity and desire to leave—only to be laid off the next week.

This power to choose which leader or organization to follow (and which one to leave behind) may not seem all that critical, but as we have said, it is the very foundation of followership. If we don't have this concept of being able to leave the leader deeply rooted in our belief system as a follower, it will eventually lead to feelings of being trapped and make our work life miserable. At the heart of a Synergetic Follower is someone who understands that they have made a conscious decision of who to follow.

If we look around we'll see numerous examples of outstanding leaders surrounded by excellent followers. I have observed this principle at work up-close in thriving local businesses, in well-run nonprofits, in educational and governmental institutions, and in successful corporations. On the other hand, we have all observed situations where there is a weak leader at the top, usually surrounded by weak followers. When an outstanding leader leaves and is replaced by someone who isn't nearly as talented, there are followers who will leave the organization (even high-paid ones)—many of them will follow the previous leader wherever they go.

The movies often depict this scenario of the follower making a choice. For example, a great warrior pledges his loyalty to the king, a well-loved, battle-worn lieutenant enlists under the service of a general, an investigator who always solves the crime agrees to help out the police chief in a tough case, or even a talented/gifted crime fighter chooses to follow and assist a caped crusader (e.g. Batman or Green Hornet). Many of the blockbuster movies of all time have great duos: Kirk and Spock, Han and Chewbacca, Jack Sparrow and Will Turner, Butch and Sundance, Thelma and Louise, Riggs and Murtaugh, and Frodo and Sam. In all these situations, the follower has made a choice to follow and the success of the leader is dependent on that choice (OK, it didn't turn out so well for Thelma and Louise). When we see a great follower choose the leader, it immediately validates and confirms the capability of the leader and our confidence grows that the leader and the follower will be successful.

As Bob Dylan reminded us, we all have to serve somebody. But who we serve (or follow) is OUR choice. Once we realize that we have the power to choose which leader to follow, we can begin to change and transform our world in a way we may never have thought possible. This realization is critical. We can only start to make a real change if we free ourselves of the chains that bind us to this leader or organization by affirming or re-affirming that we can leave if we want to. **We have a choice. In many ways, we renew and reaffirm that selection every day.**

Chapter 2
Followers and Leaders

We're going to make quite a few references to the terms "followers" and "leaders" and should define the terms from our viewpoint a little more before going any further (those two words get used and abused so much). When we refer to "follower," it is intended to mean someone who has made a choice (intentionally or un-intentionally) to follow someone who is leading—in the workplace, in a social network, as a volunteer or as part of a movement. The term "leader," is often viewed as someone who is at the top of a company or organization, but could also be a middle manager or the leader of a movement.

There are many types or styles of a follower, and a number of them are not very complimentary:

- No Clue Follower (just shows up to work, has no idea what's going on).
- Meek, Do-Whatever-the-Boss-Says Follower (AKA Minion)
- Resistant Follower (Pushes back on everything)
- Righteous Follower (Everyone at work is a captive audience for their cause)
- Complainer Follower (Every silver lining has its dark cloud)
- Brainiac Follower (Thinks he/she is smarter than everyone else. Not.)
- Mindlessly Loyal Follower (Follows without thinking)
- I-Want-to-Be-The-Boss Follower (But won't put in the effort)
- I-Should-Be-The-Boss Follower (Has no intention of putting in the effort)
- **Synergetic Follower** (More on this one in a moment)

There are many other types of followers, but the point has been made so we'll stop the list. This book is about becoming the last type of follower on the list, the Synergetic Follower. This is the type of follower who is able to change the world around them without being the leader or in charge.

One quick note. This book is NOT for the slow or minimal-effort follower. If you were hoping this book would be about how to become successful by following someone and not having to do any work, then start looking for books that are titled, "How to be Successful and Make Millions Without Trying." For those who understand that success requires effort, read on.

Synergetic Follower

Synergetic Followers are individuals who choose their leader with contemplation, careful consideration and solid commitment to work together with others to be creative, innovative and productive. It's about people who are focused on changing their part of the world. The goal is to provide authentic strength to the leader and the mission through our knowledge, skills and experience. Synergetic Followership is about changing our world while working with others to contribute significantly to the vision of the leader and the organization.

A Synergetic Follower is also someone who is more engaged than the typical worker, volunteer or employee. They are viewed as a valued colleague among their peers and often as a leader by the leader. The term refers to an individual who has consciously made a choice to follow a leader and who has little or no desire to become the leader. They use the position of follower to create change and achieve success in the organization. They are part catalyst, associate, benefactor, supporter, representative and colleague.

Synergetic Followers are sought after and recruited by leaders. The good leaders know that the key to their success is having these types of followers who work well with others and are creative, innovative, and productive. They are also the type of follower that leaders spend time and resources on to retain.

As we will see, Synergetic Followers succeed. They are highly valued, often promoted and on rare occasions become the leader (usually over their objections). If you secretly want to become the leader, then there are a thousand of books and millions of articles on leadership that will be more helpful than this one. Instead, we will talk more about resisting the opportunity to take that top leadership spot and remain as an assistant to, associate, second-in-command, close confidant or similar position in regards to the leader—and as a valued colleague and co-workers to those around you. The Synergetic Follower gains the benefit of being able to significantly influence the organization they are involved with while avoiding the visibility, distraction and pitfalls of being the top leader (leadership is not all it's made out to be).

Mindless Followers

Unfortunately, the general characterization of a follower these days is less than flattering. Today's media shouts out the benefits of being a leader and often depicts followers (minions) as mindless and weak.

An example of mindless followers can be seen in the movie Forrest Gump. Forrest, starts running across the country when he is depressed and when he reaches one coast he turns around and runs to the other coast. Along the way, people discover that he's been running a long, long time and assume he's a spiritual giant and the leader of an important movement (but in this case he's just running). Soon he has dozens of followers who are running with him all with their own ideas of why he is running. After 3 years, 2 months and 14 days, he suddenly stops and says, "I'm pretty tired . . . I think I'll go home now." His mindless followers just stare at him as they realize they've been following someone who wasn't leading them anywhere in particular. In real life, there are also a lot of people who have no idea who or why they are following, only to realize one day that the leader wasn't leading them anywhere. Usually these leaders don't have a clear picture of where they are headed either (sound familiar?).

As we'll discuss, followers don't need to be mindless or weak. In fact, when followers are active, passionate and authentic, they are the key to the leader's success. A Synergetic Follower will have a significant impact on the world around them. Leaders know that having this kind of follower helps teams, organizations and businesses to achieve the vision and goals they have set.

Followership Positions with Influence

While influence is usually attributed to leaders and is developed over time, there are actually some "follower" positions that have significant influence built into them. Often these high-impact positions are related closely to the top leader in an organization. For example, the positions below can have tremendous influence and power by the very nature of who they report to and what their duties are:

- Executive Assistant for the President or CEO of a company
- Appointment Secretary for a Governor or Mayor
- Offensive Coordinator for a football team
- Speechwriter for a public figure
- Grant writer for a well-funded nonprofit organization

In many cases, people in these types of positions don't have anyone officially reporting to them (i.e. following them from an organizational viewpoint). However, these positions not only have a lot of influence, followers in these occupations are usually very well paid and taken care of.

Another type is the single follower position. While the successful ones collaborate with others and have a lot of key relationships which help them succeed, they are usually viewed as a "follower of one." Some of these positions can have significant earnings. For example, the golf caddy who helps the successful professional golfer win in the tournaments does very well. Skilled golf caddies get paid up to 10% of the golfer's winnings plus salary. The golf caddy is a key to the golfer's success by providing their knowledge of the course, assisting with golf club selection, objective observation of the golfer's swing, and psychological support, in addition to carrying the golf bag. The successful caddy can make the difference between a golfer doing well and the golfer winning. Let's take a look at a couple golf caddy salaries: Chad Reynolds. Who? He caddies for Vijay Singh—2006 golf earnings? $510,236. Have you ever heard of Phil Mickelson's caddy, Jim MacKay? He made $445,821 in the 2006 golf season. Clearly, people who are not the leader can be paid very well. In addition, another benefit is that they can go out in public and not have to be bothered with people asking for their autograph.

Groups of Followers

It's really better if there are two or more Synergetic Followers behind a leader who work together to help the leader achieve their goals. Outstanding companies and organizations always have an excellent team behind the leader that does most of the hard work and heavy lifting in order to achieve the vision of the organization and the leader. The team usually has diverse backgrounds and skills and they have made a choice to work for and follow the leader as well as to work together as a team.

On the other hand, if this team falls apart, the performance of the whole company/organization suffers and soon the leader is looking for another company to lead. Talented leaders not only work to create successful teams, they also spend a lot of time maintaining a team of followers and keeping them together.

We don't have to look very far to find the impact of a group of Synergetic Followers. If we do a quick review of some successful leaders, Winston Churchill, Walt Disney, Martin Luther King, Abraham Lincoln, Jack Welch, Mary Kay Ash, Martha Stewart, Eleanor Roosevelt, Vince Lombardi, Nelson Mandela, Golda Meir and Oprah Winfrey—they all had an outstanding group of followers that helped them achieve their success.

It could be that one of the most successful groups of followers were the disciples of Jesus. History doesn't provide us with anything that Jesus personally wrote, but the writings of his first followers are still read and studied by millions over 2,000 years later.

When a follower or small group of followers choose to devote their time and effort to a leader can literally change the world. Our choice of who to follow should be significant, transforming and life-changing (don't forget the words of the old priest in the Indiana Jones movie who urged Dr. Jones to, "Choose wisely").

Groups of Mindless Followers

Of course, there are some who just follow without thinking or even considering that they have a choice. Popular media typically portrays this type of follower as mindless sheep that live only to please the leader. The analogy of mindless sheep was illustrated with a real life example in July of 2005 when sheepherders near Istanbul who were eating their breakfast watched as one sheep jumped off of a nearby cliff. The first sheep was followed by 1,500 more sheep that made the decision to follow the first one and also jump off the cliff to their deaths.

A more serious example of mindless followers (unless you're a sheep lover) is the mass suicide of 900 Jim Jones followers in Guyana who drank the poisoned kool-aid. Unfortunately, examples of the mindless follower are more prevalent than they should be. All we have to do is look around us at work and we will see many instances of the mindless follower (I'm sure a few individuals are coming to mind right now). The choice by many followers to "not choose" who to follow and just do the job is commonplace and constrains many organizations and businesses to mediocrity.

Impact of Leaving a Leader

What happens when people choose to leave the leader? The leader often fails or may leave as well (or is thrown out). There are plenty of movies and real-life examples where the leader makes a very public mistake or a major character flaw is exposed and as a result the followers stop following and the leader disappears quickly into anonymity.

Let's look at just one real-life example. For a brief time, Elliot Spitzer was considered an outstanding leader and defender of what is good and right. As Attorney General of New York, he brought down the famed Gambino Mafia Family, pursued securities fraud and internet fraud. There were many people across the country who loved this knight on a white horse who continued to go after the worst of the worst—the criminals and bad guys that everyone else was afraid to take on. His followers eventually helped him get elected to the office of Governor of New York in 2007. There was even talk of him someday becoming President. Then a little over a year after he was inaugurated as Governor, it was discovered that he was a regular client of a high-priced prostitution ring. While his "celebrity" increased in a negative way, his ability to lead crumbled as his followers disappeared quickly after the news broke. In fact, he resigned from office under pressure from many of his former followers and supporters. It took him several years to get back into the public eye, but it wasn't as the type of leader he had been in the past. These days, he's writing columns, providing online and TV commentary and working to establish a completely different group of followers. What happened to all of the people who worked for him and supported him? Most of them have moved on and chosen a new leader to follow. A leader is made and unmade by those who chose to follow.

Followers are as Important as Leaders

None of these observations are meant to take anything away from the leader. The leader is pivotal to any successful venture and we're always looking for more good ones. However, we often neglect the fact that followers are just as important. If we look at any sports team, it's made up of players, of teammates, of a group of individuals with different talents who combine those skills under the guidance of a coach to win. The coach doesn't have a chance at winning alone—the team is required.

Using the common analogy of a leader as the person who "steers the boat," it can be observed that steering a boat that is dead in the water is useless. The captain of the boat can turn the wheel whichever way they want, but it won't really matter if there's no one pulling on the oars and moving the boat forward. It's a requirement that something be moving in order to steer it—otherwise, they're just playing with the wheel. Without followers who are good at what they do, there is no movement regardless of which way the leader tries to steer. In some cases, we are able to observe followers who have decided not to help the leader achieve his/her goals and while there is a little movement, it is counter to the leader's direction. It won't be long before the leader in this situation is thrown overboard.

Organized Followers

When followers get organized and work together, they can be even more powerful and influential than the leader. This influence can be achieved even with a small organized group. For example in 2006 at the LA Times, the nation's second largest newspaper with 10,000 employees at the time, a small group of reporters put together a document that took on the executive management team of the LA Times multimedia division and was very critical of their online news. They put out a report that called the paper "web-stupid" and brought forward research that showed that the LA Times was far behind other online news sources.[7] The result was that the editor in charge of the multimedia division was re-assigned and the editor of the business section, who had only been in the job for a year took over the online news. That business editor, Russ Stanton, who got his start as a business reporter for the small Visalia Times-Delta newspaper, turned things around at the Times and a year later became the Editor of the LA Times. It all started with a handful of reporters.

Another example is the small team that helped design a viable fuel cell, which is beginning to power the automobile industry forward.[8] Because this group of research scientists was not restricted by the layers of bureaucracy that had slowed down or stopped other fuel research, they were able to accomplish what no one else had. They created a price-competitive alternative to the standard gas-burning engine that the world will soon depend on. As a result of their efforts, someday we may look back on their achievement the same way we viewed Thomas Edison and his small team and their discovery of a light bulb filament that stayed lit for longer than a few minutes.[9]

The Impact of Followers

A small group of organized followers with a tiny budget can sometimes accomplish near-impossible tasks which large organizations and corporations with huge resources and thousands of employees are unable to achieve. Margaret Mead reminds us, ""Never doubt that a small group of thoughtful, committed, citizens can change the world. Indeed, it is the only thing that ever has."[10] Notice that she didn't refer to a group of thoughtful, committed "leaders," because it's the followers and a leader working together that makes the real difference.

Chapter 3
Wrong Leader

As we discuss what it takes to be a Synergetic Follower, it may be that you discover that you are in the wrong organization or following the wrong leader (some have been following one for years). Instead of waiting, we're going to address some options now for those who find themselves following the wrong leader.

However, if you're convinced you're following the right leader, you should feel fortunate and may want to skip to the next chapter.

For those who are continuing because you think you might be in the wrong spot or following the wrong leader, then let's examine a few of our options. We can:

1. Leave the organization
2. Stay in the organization, but switch to a new leader
3. Stay with the same leader (and give them more time to change)
4. Become the leader

Let's inspect these options in more detail:

Leave the organization

As we mentioned before, there is great power in the realization that we "can" leave. And there are times, when staying is not the right choice. Let's ask some questions before we decide to leave.

1. Are you boxed in, unable to accomplish what you want to? Do you feel like you're wasting time staying where you're at?

2. Do you feel like you're not growing or learning and that things won't change if you stay?

3. Do you have difficulty in believing in the mission and vision of the organization?

4. Does the organization lack the leadership that convinces you that anything will change in the future?

5. Have you really tried to be a valuable follower? Have you really worked at contributing to the organization and given your best effort?

If the answer to these questions is "Yes," then it's time to seriously consider leaving. Why stay when we could choose a leader and organization where we enjoy contributing our knowledge, skills and experience and realize our goals?

Even when people realize they should choose to follow someone else, there is often hesitation for the following reasons:

1. Golden handcuffs. The promise of a big salary, retirement or other benefits that are holding us back from leaving.

2. Friends and relationships. This is a big one and is the cause for many followers to stay. But if we aren't growing and we don't believe in the leader, then maybe instead of leaving, we should meet with our colleagues and friends and figure out a way to get a new leader (legally, of course). However, if our colleagues are satisfied with the current leadership and don't want change, then we'll have to decide if the relationships we have are enough to keep us in a situation that we don't want to be in.

3. Hope that change will happen. This fits right in with our chances of buying a winning lottery ticket. In general, change happens when we do something different.

So if it's time to leave and choose another organization and leader to follow, then we need to make the decision (but don't quit just yet). Begin to seek out other organizations where the leader(s) and mission and vision do match up with who we want to follow and what we want to engage in.

Stay, but switch to a new leader

What if we believe in the mission of the organization, but we also know that we are following a bad leader or the wrong leader within it? That means it is time to ask around, do some research and find out if there is someone else that would be better to follow. The quality of leadership, even in excellent organizations, varies significantly from the worst leader to the best one.

On the other hand, the old saying, "the grass isn't greener on the other side" is often true, so we need to make our choice of whom to follow carefully and with thoughtful consideration. If we make a change without much reflection and evaluation, we may find that the new leader is actually worse than our current one (that's a scary thought).

Notice that we used the phrase "better to follow" above, instead of "easier to follow." If we follow a good or excellent leader, then our work won't necessarily be "easier," but it will be better, more satisfying and we will sense more significance and purpose in our work.

31

Organizations and businesses should be dynamic and improve in different ways all the time. If yours is not operating in this way, then that's a serious problem. It's hard to grow when the organization itself is not growing and improving. For now, let's assume we are in an organization that is dynamic and changing. If we are patient, it won't be long before an opportunity to switch leaders will present itself. As Tom Peters said, "If a window of opportunity appears, don't pull down the shade."[11] We need to be ready to make a move when that position opens up to work for the leader we want to follow.

Good leaders usually experience growth in their area, so an opportunity will come up quicker than we think. If nothing opens up, then it may be time to identify the leader we want to follow and begin to develop a relationship with him/her (platonic, of course). Over time, this relationship and others will lead to a move to their area in the future. These kinds of moves are made all the time and often don't require the opening of a new position. First-class leaders are **always** looking for excellent followers that will help improve their team and they will pick first from the pool of people they know.

Stay with the same bad leader or wrong leader

Understanding (and believing) that we are not trapped in our job can sometimes give us the confidence and energy we need to achieve our goals in spite of a less-than-optimum situation. Staying with the leader is still a valid option, but it's not a particularly enjoyable one. However, if you have thought about it and reached the decision that you "could" leave, but are consciously choosing to stay, then it may change your attitude about feeling like a victim or being trapped in your job anymore. Sometimes our viewpoint may change once we actually believe that we have the option to leave. If we apply ourselves and operate differently we can see how we could stay and be successful.

Of course, there is always a chance that the leader might change their style of leadership before we feel like we have no choice but to leave. After all, at the end of the Dickens' book, *A Christmas Carol,* Scrooge turns to his faithful worker (i.e. follower) and says, "A merrier Christmas, Bob, my good fellow, than I have given you for many a year! I'll raise your salary, and endeavor to assist your struggling family."[12] Although this tale is fictional, it could happen—some leaders do go through transformations. However, this kind of transformation is rare and sometimes requires a cataclysmic intervention by ghosts of the past, present and future.

A more likely possibility is an organizational change in leadership. Bad leaders have a way of being moved somewhere else where they can cause less damage. If we are patient and committed to being a Synergetic Follower, we may find that the leader will be moved or removed. Another common result is that someone notices our followership skills and realizes how valuable we would be and recruits us to another area.

Become the leader

Synergetic Followers make this decision all the time. Over time, they tend to pick up their own followers and eventually will have the opportunity to take over when the current leader leaves or fill a leadership position somewhere else. Just remember Yoda's quote in the movie Star Wars, "But beware of the dark side . . . If once you start down the dark path, forever will it dominate your destiny, consume you it will."[13] At the end of this book, we'll look at some famous leaders who had great followers.

One Final Caution About Leaving

Boris Groysberg, Ashish Nanda, and Nitin Nohria published a fascinating study in Harvard Business Review[14] that showed that when superstars leave and go to another business or organization, "the star's performance plunges, there is a sharp decline in the functioning of the group or team the person works with, and the company's market value falls."[15] They studied successful Wall Street analysts who left their current firm and moved to a different firm because they were attracted by things like bigger pay, more perks, an ocean view and even the perception of a better leader. Nearly half of them failed to perform at even average levels and 20% stayed that way even five years later.

If you are a successful, high-performing follower, be careful of thinking that you're solely responsible for that success and that what all the wonderful things people say about you is true. As the study by Groysber, Nanda, and Nohria shows, without our team of colleagues and co-followers, many of us will fail.

Chapter 4
Technology and Followership

It used to be that someone who followed others on a volunteer or part-time basis used mail, phone calls, money or physically showing up to help. It was more difficult back then to support more than one or two leaders or organizations that weren't part of their full-time day job.

Then email and websites came and we were able to electronically support leaders/organizations from our home computer. We could send emails advocating for the leader, encouraging others to support the organization financially and use FAQ web pages to answer questions. The rapid rise of email over the past decade has been phenomenal—nearly 1.5 billion email users worldwide.[16] But that's just the beginning.

36

Facebook, Twitter, LinkedIn and MySpace

Facebook, which was launched in 2004, now has 650 million users. Twitter, which was launched in 2006, now has nearly 200 million users. While those are the two most popular sites, there are a few other popular sites like LinkedIn, MySpace, Tagged, Orkut, and Hi5 that add a couple hundred million more users. **These social networking sites provide a powerful infrastructure for followers to influence and impact everything from a new product to overthrowing a government.**

In addition there are hundreds of thousands of smaller sites that followers use to impact the world around them. Some of these sites are specific to a nonprofit cause and are used by large nonprofits (e.g. Red Cross, United Way, Feed the Children, and American Cancer Society) and other smaller, local nonprofits. There are others that are designed for followers to support nonprofits through volunteering and philanthropy including NetworkforGood.com, VolunteerMatch.com, Giving to Charity with Change (change.com) and GlobalGiving.com. Followers can also provide microloans to entrepreneurs around the world through kiva.org.

Social networking sites like Twitter have created new "leaders" with a million followers. For example, Ashton Kutcher, former star of *That 70's Show,* and a star in B-movies like

Dude, Where's My Car and *What Happens in Vegas,* should be just another character actor. But he has somehow parlayed his background and personality on Twitter to gather over 7 million followers, who are captured by his everyday thoughts and actions. To his credit, he has used his leadership on Twitter to influence his followers to join him in his efforts to stop human trafficking.

It's easy for a "follower" on Twitter to follow or un-follow an individual and millions of Twitter followers make decisions about who they follow every day. Today, this online "following" is a lot less risky and involves no commitment. As this social networking technology evolves during the next few years it will give followers an increasingly stronger voice and influence and require a greater commitment.

Overthrow Governments?

There are many conflicting opinions on whether social networking sites like Facebook and Twitter helped followers overthrow foreign governments.[17] One thing is clear, followers utilized those sites to communicate with each other in ways that had never been done before to overthrow (or nearly overthrow) the current government. These new tools that are still in their infancy (they are only 5-6 years old), are having a huge impact on society and on followers' ability to organize, communicate and choose leaders and movements to support. The impact of sites like these built on current technology will only increase as social networking matures.

Technology, specifically social networking sites, smart phones, and tablets/pads/slates are giving followers increasing influence and a variety of choices of leaders to follow that they have never had before. While most of this book is oriented towards "Who you choose to follow" as your primary full-time vocation—most of the concepts also apply to this rapidly growing world of online, part-time/volunteer following.

Chapter 5
Having more influence than the Leader

In general, the leader is the one with the influence in an organization, but in some situations a follower can actually have more influence than their leader. There are leaders who are good at leading the organization, but still don't have the influence that one of their followers have. This can create conflict as the people around the leader and the follower can be confused as to who the "true" leader is.

The point could be made that an "influential" follower might also be a leader in their own right—which happens occasionally. They will find that they have followers of their own and occasionally from leaders and followers in other areas.

For example, Linus Torvalds works for the Linux Foundation and reports to the Executive Director, but he is someone who has thousands of followers. He is from Helsinki, Finland and created the Linux operating system, which was his own open source version of UNIX.[18] For a number of years, he was a "fellow" for a chip-making company and is now a fellow at the Linux Foundation working on ways to make Linux better. In the corporate world, a "fellow" is a designation given to a few top non-management researchers or scientists who work on special projects funded by the corporation and often don't have anyone directly reporting to them.

Even though the foundation is small and they only have a few employees, when Linus shows up at Linux conferences around the world he is treated like a rockstar with hundreds of Linux fans asking for his autograph. His sphere of influence exceeds that of the Executive Director of the foundation.[19] To the Executive Director's credit, he realizes the strength of having someone like Linus working for the organization and doesn't compete with his influence.

Followers often stay longer than the leader

It's common for followers to have longer careers in an organization or business compared to their leaders. Long-term leaders at the top are rare. The spotlight and pressures have a tendency to burn top leaders out much quicker than followers. CEOs of Fortune 500 Companies are getting younger and younger and only 50% have been in their position for 3 years or more.[20] Average tenure for CEOs at most smaller companies is even shorter. History has shown us that it is extremely rare for a CEO to hold that position for more than a decade. In contrast, many of the staff in large companies or organizations have been there for 20-30 years.

For instance, many of the staff of a large government office with an elected leader have been there for years despite the revolving door of the leader. When a new leader is elected, he/she will bring in a few of their trusted friends to help with policy-setting and maybe some high-level operations, but they will keep most of the frontline staff and others who already know the work and have all the contacts for getting the work done. I remember visiting a governmental office in Washington D.C. and trying to get a feel for the political leanings of a top staff member. She kept saying, "*This* administration believes . . ." or "*This* administration has chosen to . . ." She wasn't going to identify her politics, because in that situation it didn't matter (plus it is much safer not to). Many of these key staffers have seen several different "administrations" come through and have outlasted them by working hard and following the politics of the current leader.

There's always pressure to succeed quickly for an elected official, especially with the increased focus on the first 100 days in office. If you were elected into office and had four years to show that the people were right in electing you, then you don't have the time to learn everything that's necessary for success. Keeping the key staff who have been there and willing to support your politics is very helpful. If the leader doesn't keep some of the key staff (i.e. followers), they won't be able to develop the contacts and processes necessary to get things done fast enough to be successful.

Followers Change the World

The truth is that being a Synergetic Follower is an incredible vocation. We agree that leaders are important, but leaders can't be successful without the followers who choose to follow. **Great companies require both top level leadership and top level followership. Without great followers, there are no great leaders.** So while the leaders get the tough high-level decisions, the corner office and a higher salary, it is the followers who do the heavy lifting and help the organization be successful.

Our first decision towards success is **choosing** the leader.

Chapter 6
Benefits to Synergetic Followership

The leader-follower relationship is often viewed as a one-way relationship, that is, the leader requests and the follower does the work. However, Synergetic Followers achieve considerably more than that in their relationships (and so do successful leaders). **In the best situation, Synergetic Followers create a win-win environment where the leader and the follower both gain from the relationship.** It's worth mentioning a few benefits here.

Learning

A major benefit of choosing a good leader to follow is the wisdom and knowledge that can be gained. Much can be learned by observing the leader's example, listening to what they say about different topics, watching how they overcome challenges and face crises, seeing how they handle stress and difficult people, and observing how they lead and influence others. It's important to pay attention to the leader and reflect on what the leader does and how they handle difficult situations. Learning from the leader will also help us work more effectively with them. As a result, we'll know how they will react in situations and can complement or balance their actions.

In addition, there aren't any "born leaders." All leaders used to follow someone in the beginning of their career (except for a few young dictators who inherited the job). The type of learning that comes from observing the leader grow and mature is invaluable—even if we never choose to be a leader ourselves.

Challenging Work

Looking for challenges is a character trait of the Synergetic Follower, who also recognizes that attainment of goals is never easy. If our aim is to just do the minimal level work for the leader and not to stretch ourselves, then we will achieve the easy-to-reach goal of mediocrity. Thomas Edison said, "Opportunity is missed by most because it is dressed in overalls and looks like work."[21] The Synergetic Follower enjoys the challenge to achieve above and beyond the "meets minimum standards" required of the job description. They labor to set a new maximum level of behavior, effort and achievement.

Accomplishment

Hard work and challenging projects are fundamental to achieving worthy goals. However, there should also be a sense of accomplishment and growth that comes with the blood, sweat and tears. Success story after success story shows us that "overnight success" is rare. Most of the time success comes from years of persistence, difficult effort, lots of failure and many small wins. The work we do and the time we invest should have significance. We should have an awareness that the world is being changed or transformed (or at least a small part of it) through our efforts and contribution. If all of the hard work doesn't result in the attainment of our goals and the leader's goals, then we're not much different than the rest of the followers (except that we're working harder than they are). John Wooden said simply, "Never mistake activity for achievement."[22] **Although effort and working with others towards a goal is important—accomplishment and real results are critical to being a Synergetic Follower.**

Leadership

In many cases, the Synergetic Follower will also be involved in leading others (officially or unofficially). A great deal can be learned from being both a follower and a leader at the same time. Synergetic Followers are approached on a regular basis to lead a project or team. And some followers even enjoy being a leader so much that they eventually switch to full-time leadership. However, most of the time they are completely satisfied with changing the world as a member of a successful team without being in charge (we've got more than enough people who think they are leaders). In the past, business success was determined by how many people reported to us, but times have changed. In this age of collaborative and team-oriented effort, there are many success stories that are linked to followers working together with other followers. And in today's world we have crowdstorming and crowdsourcing where nearly anonymous followers work together through a social network to accomplish work.

Influence

The Synergetic Follower also has influence on others around them. We have already given several examples of followers who have a significant influence over the efforts of others, but who don't directly report to them or are on a peer level with them. Scott Adams, who created the cartoon, *Dilbert*, says, "You don't have to be a 'person of influence' to be influential. In fact, the most influential people in my life are probably not even aware of the things they've taught me." [23]

As we've mentioned, a lot of work today is being done in

teams and as a follower we can be a strong influence on the results the team produces. There are also many assistants and experts and professionals who don't have staff reporting to them, but wield a great deal of influence. For example, the Deputy Secretary for Appointments for the Governor of New York has tremendous power and influence. Without having a bunch of people reporting to them, the follower in this position influences who gets in to see the Governor, where the Governor gives speeches and what events the Governor shows up at. An additional example is the Twitter world where Neil deGrasse Tyson, an astrophysicist with the Hayden Planetarium, is followed by over 150,000 people.[24] Neil (@neiltyson) educates and influences a mass of people through the medium of 140-character posts on space, black holes, planets, space shuttles and UFOs.

Paycheck

One of the fundamental benefits we receive for working for someone is a paycheck. Unfortunately, it's often what many people portray as the main reason to work. Contrary to its perceived importance, surveys show that the amount of the salary is not in the top three priorities of people's list for staying in a job.[25] If the primary reason we are working in our current position is to get a paycheck, then we're truly just "working" for someone and we're not operating as a Synergetic Follower. **While our job is what pays the bills, we** should work where we can be passionate about what we do and the positive impact the contributions our business or organization is making on the world around us. While a paycheck is a fundamental benefit of working for someone, it is lower on the priority list of most followers. If we can't stop thinking about our pay (or lack of it), then either we're too obsessed with making money or it's an indicator that we might be in the wrong spot and the time has come to find a new position and a new leader. We can't be a Synergetic Follower if our thoughts are occupied by our financial compensation.

Change the World

The final benefit that we'll mention is the ultimate goal of the Synergetic Follower—to change or transform our world, without being the top leader. We work with our colleagues and drive forward with the expectation of being successful. **Failure is part of the process towards any major successful goal, but it's not meant to stop us. Failure is supposed to help us learn, mature and test us.** In the book, *The Road to Success is Paved with Failure*, the author Joey Green reminds us, "Just remember, everyone falls down. You're not a failure until you don't get back up."[26] Growth and learning from "falling down" is instructive and helpful for future projects, but the Synergetic Follower has to keep getting back up. The attainment of our goals in addition to the goals of the business and the leader is the key result that keeps the Synergetic Follower going for the long term. When those goals are achieved, we have truly succeeded and made another step towards changing our world.

Chapter 7
Some Wrong Reasons to Follow

Although there are many benefits and compelling reasons to follow a leader, there are a few wrong reasons to follow. Many of these will actually hold us back from being a Synergetic Follower, including these JB's:

Just Because . . .

- They give us a paycheck
- They are rich and influential
- They are popular and have lots of friends
- Our friends or colleagues follow
- We like the perks
- Finding a new leader would be too much work

In reality, people frequently choose leaders for any and all of the above (and for even worse reasons). But these motives reduce followership down to a more base level and are not the motivation for a Synergetic Follower to follow a leader. These types of reasons don't usually lead anywhere and rarely anything of significance gets accomplished (except by accident).

Synergetic Followers are less focused on themselves and more focused on working together with others to accomplish goals that lead to transformation or significant changes. John Wooden, the legendary basketball coach said, "You can't live a perfect day without doing something for someone who will never be able to repay you." [27]

The list of wrong reasons for following listed above are distracting and take our eyes off of the mission of the organization. Our motivation for being in the position that we're in should be that we are compelled by the vision and leadership of the leader and want to work together with others to make a significant contribution to that vision.

In addition, most good leaders can spot someone who is following for the more self-serving reasons listed above. It may satisfy a specific need for the leader for a short time to have a follower or two like that. But once the leader recognizes that the individual is following for the wrong (or self-serving) reasons including the ones listed above, they will usually work quickly to transfer the individual to another position or to limit their influence.

While we're at it, let's look at three other types of followers that most leaders prefer not to have: Fans, Creepy Followers, and Puppy Dog Followers.

Fans

Fans mostly follow stars, not leaders. There is a big difference between a Synergetic Follower and a fan (or groupie). A fan can be an enthusiastic devotee of the organization or leader and in rare cases can help move an organization or company forward. However, the fan's motivation is usually to be closer to the leader and be associated with him or her, not to be a significant contributing part of the movement. Usually they prefer to sit on the bench, cheer on the leader and be close to the action. It's not a bad thing to be a fan, it just isn't what we're calling Synergetic Followership. Plus, there are those fans that have ulterior motives and desire to be close to the leader hoping that some of the leader's success rubs off on them.

Creepy Followers

This is a fan that is a little stranger than the others. Someone who follows a little too close and whose behavior might be a little weird or creepy (they make movies about these types of followers). Remember when we used to call people like this "secret admirers?" Anything that causes someone to appear like a stalker (hanging around too closely or at the wrong time or in the wrong way) will not be welcomed by the leader.

In his book, *Illusions of Immortality: A Psychology of Fame and Celebrity*, David Giles states, "the difference between a devotee and a stalker might be that the latter carries an implied threat of violence (or at least of extremely unpredictable and/or disturbing behaviour)."[28] These days, creepy followers have cameras and are spooky and potentially dangerous. Even though we may love following the leader we've chosen—let's keep it professional.

Puppy-dog Followers

These individuals tend to be over-enthusiastic and are excited just to be in the leader's presence. They follow the leader's every word and action, they look for praise often (or a pat on the head), and are constantly seeking to help the leader (yes, it sounds like a groupie). While some leaders may enjoy this in the beginning, it soon begins to be annoying. It won't be long before the leader will start to avoid the Puppy-dog Follower. In addition, this type of behavior tends to have a negative effect on colleagues and peers who will quickly spot Puppy-dog Followers and will seek to remove them immediately.

Now that we've examined a number of reasons why we should and should not follow a leader, we're almost ready to move on and look at what makes a Synergetic Follower. But before we do, with so many bad leaders out there (and everyone is bound to work for a couple of them over their career), we're going to take a closer look at what to do if we find ourselves working for one of them.

Chapter 8
What If We Are Following a Bad Leader?

There are relatively few good leaders in the world compared to the proliferation of average leaders and the seemingly endless list of bad leaders. We can **thrive** under a good leader, we can **live** under an average one, but we can only **survive** under a bad leader. Barbara Kellerman wrote an entire book on bad leaders, where she describes the range of bad leaders, "I set up a continuum in which the first type of bad leadership, incompetence, is far less onerous than the last type of bad leadership, evil."[29]

Here's a classic quote from a bad boss, "I didn't say it was your fault. I said I was going to blame it on you." If we are one of the unfortunate souls who reports to a bad leader (and very few make it through life without having at least one), what can we do? There are several approaches to dealing with a bad leader, let's examine five of them:

1. Succeed Anyway
2. How Bad is the Bad Leader Really
3. Bad Leaders Get Fired
4. Bad Leaders Get Reassigned
5. Bad Leaders are Worse Than Bad Jobs.

Succeed Anyway

Although it's more challenging, many great things have been accomplished in spite of a bad leader. Just because our leader is the spawn of the devil, doesn't mean that we can't accomplish the goals that we want to. However, it's going to be more difficult and likely a lot less fun than if we were with a great leader.

The good news is that a bad leader is frequently in a job that exceeds their knowledge and skills (e.g. Peter Principle and the Dilbert Principle). This pressure can result in the bad leader being so focused on trying to keep their position of power that they don't pay as much attention to what's going on around them (including what their followers are doing). This self-focus of a bad leader can be tough to work with, but it can create a situation which will allow us some freedom to get our goals done, while they aren't paying attention.

How Bad Is The Bad Leader?

When following a bad leader, it's not uncommon to think about how nice it would be to follow a good leader or even an average one. However, that's when the old saying comes back to haunt us, "The grass isn't always greener on the other side of the fence." In fact, as we've all found out, the grass on the other side can be browner or even dead. This common expression helps us remember that we could leave a bad boss and end up following a horrible one. As Kellerman mentioned, bad leaders range from incompetent to evil. Everything has risk—including leaving a bad leader.

Bad Leaders Get Fired

Bad leaders are often self-destructive and sometimes if we'll just be a little patient, they'll blow themselves up without any help from us. We don't have to think too far back to find famous examples: Richard Nixon, Kenneth Lay (Enron), John Edwards, Bernie Madoff, Michael Brown (head of FEMA during Hurricane Katrina), Elliot Spitzer, and many, many others. I'm sure if we take just a few moments, we can come up with some of our own personal stories where a bad boss made a huge mistake and was fired or forced to resign.

Bad Leaders Get Reassigned

One more thought. Even if they don't mess up in a way that gets them fired, bad leaders still can be reassigned to some remote part of the company or country (and often are). In a government/education institution, where it's nearly impossible to fire someone incompetent, it is still possible to get them reassigned to some other department or area (perhaps in a cold part of the world) that can better appreciate their limited set of skills and knowledge. In rare cases, they are promoted in order to keep them from getting in the way of a team that is accomplishing something important. This strategy was highlighted by Scott Adams in *The Dilbert Principle*, "The basic concept of the Dilbert Principle is that the most ineffective workers are systematically moved to the place where they can do the least damage: management."[30]

Bad Leaders are Worse Than Bad Jobs

Surveys have shown that people tend to leave a job because they have a bad leader, not because it's a bad job. For anyone who has ever worked for a bad leader, the results of the surveys make sense—working for a bad leader is miserable. Most of us have worked for at least one bad leader and the more unfortunate among us have worked for several. These leaders have many recognizable traits that usually make us want to follow someone else. Anyone else!

In the next chapter we'll identify some of those traits—I'm sure you'll have some of your own to add to the list.

Despite our discussion about bad leaders, most of them are not intentionally bad. Most of them are former followers who were promoted or hired into leadership positions beyond their capacity to lead. Some are struggling to learn on the job and as a result of their desire to grow, they will likely improve over time (if we are patient). Most leaders are average (or mediocre) and don't produce a lot of success or create much damage. But the smaller group of bad leaders can cause a lot of damage, which is why we'll spend the next chapter talking about how to deal with them.

Chapter 9
The Top Ten Bad Leader Traits

Our ability to be a Synergetic Follower can be impacted by the traits of a bad leader. It's important to recognize what they are, in order to create "work-around" methods to deal with them or alternatively to choose another leader.

1. They are more concerned about themselves than others

The terms "self-absorbed and "selfish" come to mind—and it is usually an understatement as to how these leaders behave. They always seem to have a mirror nearby and they save any piece of paper, email or voicemail that might say something nice about them. All of their stories seem to be about themselves (Yawn). Every conversation, no matter how it starts out, begins to turn ever so slowly (or quickly) to be about them. Benjamin Franklin said, "People wrapped up in themselves make very small packages." These types of leaders are truly small packages, but can create a mountain of problems. It's not so much that they don't like others, they just love themselves. They are completely preoccupied and fascinated with who they are. Don't ever expect them to notice you, except in passing, much the same way that a celebrity notices a fan.

2. They value things above people

There are a lot of bad leaders who value things like money, position, car, office size, the view from the window, golf clubs and a parking space over people. Some bad leaders actually do value people, as long as those people help them get more things. These types of leaders believe that people are just human *resources* (with a big emphasis on the word "resources"). In other words, people are just additional "things" to have. The rules are fairly simple when working for these types of leaders, be as valuable as you can and prepare for the day when they get tired of you (like they do with their golf clubs). This is the opposite of good leaders, who realize that their followers are the real reason for their success.

3. *They are unable to be ethical or loyal*

The disconnection from integrity and morality is common among bad leaders. As the character J.R. Ewing said on the old TV show, *Dallas*, "Once integrity goes, the rest is a piece of cake." Any perceived loyalty from this type of bad leader is a misperception and always momentary in nature. Most of these bad leaders who are unethical have rationalized themselves into believing that what they do somehow makes sense (which is easier if they view themselves as the center of the earth). A Walker Information study showed that, "79 percent of employees who questioned their bosses' integrity said they felt trapped at work or uncommitted or were likely to leave their jobs soon."[31]

Since everything revolves around this type of bad leader, then laws are for everyone else and exceptions are justified for them. Even if that means violating a trust, lying to others or pretending to be something they are not.

The good news is that their behavior and actions are very predictable. **We can completely trust that they will do whatever is in their own best interests regardless of who it hurts or what laws or rules of ethics it violates.** Understanding this basic truth will help us navigate through the work day with the unethical leader.

4. They believe their job title makes them a leader

Bad leaders often believe that their job title is proof that they are a leader and that others will be compelled to follow them as a result of their position in the organization. This is more commonly referred to as "positional authority." People who parade their positional authority with an air of superiority rarely command the admiration they think they're getting. A friend of mine refers to a leader like this as "someone who was born on third base and thinks they hit a triple."

Respect is earned—it is not given by promoting someone or changing the words on their business card. These types of leaders are usually in a position that exceeds their capability. Some of them even realize that they are in a position that is above them. The upside for having a positional leader who recognizes they are in over their head is that they are very appreciative of anyone who helps them succeed—as long as the appropriate deference is given to them according to their job title.

Side Note: On the other hand, good leaders can be found with almost any title or no title. These types of leaders rarely mention their title and people follow because they are a true leader, not because they have a title. Think of some of the movies with leadership types of characters. In many cases they didn't really have a title or positional authority:

Schindler in *Schindler's List*, Frodo in *"The Lord of the Rings*, the archeology professor in *Indiana Jones*, Forrest in *Forrest Gump*, Jake in *Avatar*. While these characters weren't official- ly given authority as a leader, they had the respect of those who followed them and we cheered them on anyway.

5. They fear competition from others

Napoleon Hill, in the classic 1937 motivational book, *Think and Grow Rich*, said, "The leader who fears that one of his followers may take his position is practically sure to realize that fear sooner or later."[32] Paranoia can be self-fulfilling and we need to avoid these types of leaders whenever possible. Even if we work hard as a follower, this type of leader will view our hard work as an effort to eventually replace them. This leader's world is filled with the perception that everyone really is out to get them. It makes them incredibly difficult to work with, because many of the things we do are viewed with the assumption that we are trying to undercut the lead- er. Good efforts just look like we're showing off or laying the groundwork for a promotion or trying to attract the atten- tion of someone above the paranoid leader.

As a result, nothing we do will be appreciated or taken the way we intended. The only way to survive a leader like this is to do our work well (but not so that it stands out to everyone) and give the leader all or most of the credit. But in some cases the paranoia is so severe, that it still won't be long before you find that you've been fired or re-assigned somewhere else to reduce the misguided threat this leader perceives you to be.

6. *They lack humility*

The phrase, "lack of humility," is a nice way of saying this type of leader is "ego-driven." This is similar to #1 above, "They are more concerned about themselves than others." **Humility is one of the character traits we admire most in great leaders and it's the one we least expect in bad leaders.** If we find ourselves following a leader who lacks humility, then it puts us in a situation where we will be encouraged to make it appear that every good idea, action, or outcome came from the leader. For the ego-driven leader, followers are just an extension of the leader, they don't exist for any other purpose. In the hands of an ego-driven leader, followers are like a rake or a steering wheel—just an inanimate object that they use to accomplish their goals. This type of bad leader is still better than the leader we just mentioned who fears competition. This one takes all the credit anyway, so there's no need to worry about trying to avoid seeking credit (more on that later).

7. *They are disconnected from reality*

This type of bad leader just doesn't get it. They don't understand what others are doing (or why they are doing it), they don't understand what makes things work—they don't even understand themselves. We just shake our heads and wonder how they fell into the position they are in, because it must have been an accident (or a relative). Often the problem can be tied to a center-of-the-universe problem, where the leader thinks that everything revolves around them. This can cause a disconnection from reality, because they are the only ones that have that belief.

Fortunately, the "disconnected-from-reality" leader doesn't last too long. Sooner or later they will make a critical decision based on that disconnection that will be too obvious for those above to ignore and they will fire the leader or move them to some remote outpost of the organization where a connection to reality isn't needed. Patience is key with this type of leader as well as continual communication about reality (in a positive way). It's also important to keep documentation, lots of documentation about everything.

8. *They believe that life is a zero-sum game*

Some leaders feel like they've lost something when someone else succeeds at a project or goal, even if they are not involved in the project. This is commonly referred to zero-sum thinking. As Rich Karlgaard reminds us, the media encourages zero-sum thinking, "Television, vile on so many levels, is a carrier of the zero-sum disease: There is only one Survivor, one American Idol and a single-digit number who escape

Donald Trump's wagging finger."[33] Sports and other competitive environments can also promote this sort of thinking as well with slogans like, "winning is everything" and "there can only be one winner."

The opposite of zero-sum thinking is "win-win" or abundance thinking, which is an approach many great leaders have. This is the idea that there can be two or more winners in a situation, not just one. If we find ourselves with a zero-sum leader, then competition will rule the day. In this situation there will be winners and there will always be losers. Every day is a competition against others in the team (which doesn't really promote teamwork). Therefore the team breaks down as each teammate becomes a sole performer.

9. They can be volatile and lack consistency

One of the worst types of leaders is the "volatile" one. This is the leader who flies off the handle for unpredictable reasons. People walk around them like they are treading on thin ice waiting for the ice to break and swallow them up at any moment. In fact, even in the face of success, this type of bad leader will find something to blow up about. It creates a very risk-averse work environment, because no one wants to be the cause of the boss being upset.

This type of trait in bad leaders creates situations where we never know what to expect. It's difficult to work in an environment where nothing can be predicted or where the leader explodes when everyone least expects it. This is one of the worst forms of a bad leader and few can stomach it. Stay calm if possible, do the work well, meet deadlines, and try to stay out of the way. If we realize we are following this type of leader, we should begin planning our exit strategy.

10. Constantly Critical

There are those that experienced a childhood of criticism, where nothing they ever did was right. It is one of the benefits of growing up because there's an opportunity to leave the constant criticism behind. With the "constantly critical" type of boss, we get to have that childhood feeling back—only without the love. The constantly critical leader chases away good followers and ends up keeping those who have no other option or who like being micromanaged and enjoy the feeling of being criticized and about everything they do. Some of these followers are the same people who often are critical of themselves as well (they sound a lot like Eeyore from the "Winnie the Pooh" stories). These types of followers have given up all hope assume their life will be full of criticism and punishment.

For the rest of us, we look forward to when this type of leader is on vacation or sick—those are the good days (it's similar to the relief we feel when we stop pounding our head on the table). It takes strong internal confidence and self-awareness to survive this type of leader. If that doesn't describe you, then perhaps it's time to start looking for a position elsewhere.

Good Leader, but the Wrong One

We've just spent time talking about bad leaders, but there are some situations, where the leader is good. However, they are just the wrong one for us and we may find that we choose to leave just because there isn't a good match. **There are many different styles of leadership that can be successful, but it may be that the one our leader utilizes doesn't fit our style of followership.** In other very rare situations, the leader may have some personality tick that annoys us so much we can't bear to work with them (like body odor that is overwhelming, talking baby-talk when illustrating a point or constantly doing lame celebrity impressions). Still, it's better to put up with these "personality ticks," if the leader is one who inspires us and provides the vision and direction that we believe in. The reality is that if these types of things bother us, we probably are having trouble buying into the organization and leader and need to re-evaluate who we are following.

Since working with a good leader is not common, if we have a chance to work with one, we should overlook many things in order to stay. There isn't much that is worse than a bad leader—even bad body odor is easier to overcome than leadership that stinks.

Chapter 10
The Default Follower

The opposite of a Synergetic Follower is the Default Follower. **The Default Follower is someone who is in a job they didn't really choose or someone who continues to follow a leader they don't really want to follow.** We use the term *follow* very loosely in this case. In reality, the "Default Follower" is just going through the motions, showing up most days and working for whoever happens to be in charge. This condition can happen by accident sometimes, because the circumstances of who we report to aren't always under our control. We can find ourselves suddenly working for someone we didn't choose and don't really want to follow. If we think about the statistics, this can happen to all of us since there aren't that many good leaders compared to all the average or mediocre ones (and of course, more bad leaders than we deserve).

How do we know if we are a Default Follower? It's usually a follower who has one or more of the thoughts below. In the beginning they might have even said the following statements out loud, but now they just drag themselves through work like a modern-day zombie muttering them to no one in particular:

- I feel trapped in my current position. I can't get out.
- I wish I could follow someone else.
- I don't respect my leader.
- What were they thinking when they put my boss in charge?
- I could do a better job than my manager does.
- The leadership in this organization has no clue.

At the start there was a sense of being trapped, but they have complained quietly for so long that the situation now feels normal. Somehow they have grown accustomed to their cage. The Default Follower has given up. Maybe at one time they had a drive for something better, but it's gone now.

Let's take a look at these Default Follower questions/statements in a little more detail:

"I feel trapped in my current position"

It could be that as we examine our current job we see that our career path has no future and there appears to be no chance of being promoted during the upcoming decade. It might even be the result of a micromanager who is always hovering nearby reminding us of our faults. This "caged animal" feeling makes work miserable. In the wild, an animal is willing to chew off their leg if it is caught in a trap. In the workplace, there are people who would do the same thing if they could gain freedom.

Alex Pattakos, in his book about Viktor Frankl's principles said, "In addition to the feelings of inner emptiness that seem to exist among greater numbers of our working (and, for that matter, retired) population, more people feel trapped at work—and perhaps in life generally."[34] For these followers, every day is a challenge to get out of bed and go to work.

"I wish I could follow someone else"

This is likely a statement from someone who has given up (and feels trapped). The "I wish . . . " phrase at the beginning of the statement indicates that the person has settled into a sad fairy tale, 'wishing' for something better, but accepting that their prince (or princess) will never come. Unfortunately, in many organizations, there are so many average/mediocre leaders, that there isn't a lot for a person to choose from.

However, if we look hard enough (and maybe lower our standards just a bit), it could be that there is a real-life example of a good leader nearby that is better than the current one. Don't give up hope and sink into whining, no matter how bad a leader you have. As followers we have the choice to follow who we want to. If we don't see anything nearby, it just means we're going to have to look harder and increase the scope of our search.

"I don't respect my leader"

The ability to respect our leader is a foundational concept for a Synergetic Follower—it is required. Now that doesn't mean that we have to agree with everything our leader says or does, but without respect it's nearly impossible to be the kind of follower we want to be. The dictionary defines *respect* as "esteem for or a sense of the worth or excellence of a person, a personal quality or ability." In other words, we "value" the leader and the qualities the leader has. It doesn't have to do with their personality or style.

Respect is a key part of why we made the choice to follow. If we don't respect them, then we are likely a Default Follower. In that case we haven't made a choice yet, we're just working for them. John Baldoni spoke about what happens when there is no respect, "And when people have no respect for their leader, this often compromises their performance, ie, they may not do as well as they would if they were more motivated."[35] We know it to be true—if we don't have respect for our leader (or have lost the respect we had), it's time to move on. Let's seek out and select a leader we can respect.

"Why did they put my boss in charge?"

This completely bypasses the distaste we have for our leader and indicates that we don't even have a positive opinion about the leaders above our leader. In other words, our leader is so bad that whoever put them in charge has also lost our respect. We can't figure out why we're the only ones that have noticed how bad our leader is and can only assume that other leaders in the business are just as bad.

If we are having these kinds of thoughts, then we are quickly moving to the place where we are giving up on the whole organization, falling into a state of despair, and beginning to lose hope that anything will ever be different. We're convinced that if our boss is ever replaced, it will likely be with someone just as bad. It's time to start looking outside the organization for someone to follow. Someone that deserves our talents, knowledge, experience, and will appreciate the significant contribution we will make.

"I could do a better job"

This statement indicates that we believe that the leader is inept at leading and that we could make better decisions than the leader does. We're really just beginning to imagine that we could make a better leader. This could be the result of two things: the leader is so bad that even a follower would be a better leader. Or it could be that our own leadership skills are developing and we're beginning to realize our potential as a leader, especially when we see how bad the current leadership is. The problem is that the latter sentiment can lead to the fulfillment of those thoughts. We could end up replacing our leader when the higher level leaders remove him or her.

Look what happened to Rudy Giuliani. Back in May of 1987 he was an US attorney in New York prosecuting Wall Street execs like Ivan Boesky. When New York magazine asked him how he felt about CEOs who resented him for telling them how to run their company, he said, "That's because probably I could do a better job of it. I'm probably considerably more intelligent, much more creative, much better able to run things than lots of people do."[36] It wasn't too long after that that the City of New York elected him to run their city.

If we're not ready for leadership or don't want to be the leader, then we need to focus on our followership skills that relate to a bad leader or select another leader that we think would do a better job than we would.

One note on this idea—the world is filled with people that think they can do better than their leader. This is not what a

Synergetic Follower is about. **If we choose to stay, we want to work with the leader, sometimes in spite of their inability to lead, in order to accomplish great things.**

"The leaders in this organization have no clue"

This is similar to the previous statements, except it clearly states a lack of faith in all of the leadership and the direction the company or organization is taking, not just a single leader. But instead of leaving and choosing another leader, the Default Follower stays and has chosen to collect a paycheck and play the victim. Even if there is a good leader somewhere in the organization, they are lumped into the group of non-performing, no-clue leaders. Unfortunately, in many companies, this is the status quo for many followers. As a result, it creates a situation where it is difficult for leaders to lead and for followers to follow. In a successful organization or company, leaders lead and followers have made the choice to stay and follow.

How People Become a Default Follower

It's easy to become a Default Follower—don't do anything except the minimum. Just go where you're told to go, report to who they assign you to, do the least amount of work required, and don't think of things ever being better. There are a lot of people who think this level of followership is the standard. That doesn't mean Default Followers don't have to work hard. In fact, there are a lot of them who work very hard and go where they are told to go. There is no escape for this type of follower, because they don't believe they have a choice. Default Followers tend to be a bit fatalistic and can sound like victims. They believe that what they get and who they report to is pre-determined and they can't do anything about it. They often sabotage their success and begin whining from the very beginning, as Seth Godin said in a recent blog,

> "Amazingly, we often look for the excuse before we even accept the project. We say to ourselves, "well, I can start this, and if it doesn't work perfectly, I can point out it was the . . . " Then, as the team ramps up, bosses appear and events occur (or not), we continually add to and refine our excuse list, reminding ourselves of all the factors that were out of our control."[37]

The Default Follower's style of work will usually result in a paycheck, but little else. For those who are looking for more than a paycheck, read on.

Chapter 11
Ten Components of a Synergetic Follower

Now that we've decided to follow our leader (or have left our old leader and found a new one we believe in), let's look more closely at what it takes to be a Synergetic Follower. The foundation, as we've mentioned, is the choice to work with others in a creative, innovative, and productive manner. It's an attitude that recognizes we have something to contribute to the success of the organization and our leader. Becoming this type of follower requires the development of a number of traits and skills.

There are ten components that are necessary for a Synergetic Follower:

1. Believe in the Mission and the Leader
2. Team Work
3. Seek Diversity of Strengths
4. Just Do It
5. Don't Seek Credit
6. Build Trust
7. Active Followership
8. Managing Up
9. Communicate and Handle Conflict
10. Make Decisions Based on Data

We're going to cover these ten components in more detail in the next few chapters, but it's worth doing a brief overview of them. The first component is foundational. No follower will be truly successful without believing in the mission and the leader. The rest of the components are not in any specific order in regards to importance. Synergetic Followers all have some level of each component.

One. Believe in the Mission and the Leader

Let's look at the Mission first. If we don't buy into the mission of the organization or company or the movement or effort that we are engaged in then we need to stop and rethink why we are there. In reality, many people find themselves engaged in some effort either in a job or as a volunteer and never really think about why they are there or if it fits with their life goals.

In addition to believing in the Mission, it is essential that we decide if the leader that we are following is the right one for us. This is important especially if the organization is small and only has one person in a leadership/management role. In most small organizations, the leader and the mission become one and the same and if we don't believe in one, we probably won't believe in the other. Another challenge with a small organization with only one leader is: if we don't like the leader, there's no one else to follow. Large organizations have their own unique challenges, but they do offer more leaders to choose from.

Two. Team Work

It used to be that working independently inside an organization was the norm. But times have changed and these days, work is a team sport. There are still some companies that operate with a focus on the single, independent worker, but today the most successful organizations have strong teams and their people work collaboratively. For success, a team-orientation also requires many of the other components including integrity, humility, diversity, and communication.

Three. Seek Diversity of Strengths

Seeking diversity of strengths has some similarities with the team-oriented approach. **It means looking at our strengths, instead of our weaknesses.** Every challenge or problem or crisis that comes along can also be viewed as an opportunity. Every situation or person that we work with, even the "worst" ones still have opportunities and strengths that can be utilized to succeed.

It also refers to the strength of diversity. People often think of diversity as a disadvantage when putting together a team as an additional challenge that will have to be overcome. But diversity brings strength to a team and is a key ingredient in successful projects. The best teams include people with different backgrounds, different skills, different cultures and different abilities.

Four. Just Do It

The third component of the definition of the word "synergetic" is being productive. This means to stop talking and discussing and researching—and follow the instructions of the famous Nike slogan, "Just Do It." Research, planning, and design are all keys for a successful project, but we have to actually implement, ship, deliver or complete the project or we won't be successful. Like the book title (and book), *Getting Things Done* by David Allen, the Synergetic Follower understands the concept of being productive and of getting things done.

Five. Don't Seek Credit

The Synergetic Follower does not seek or claim credit for the accomplishments of the team. Being humble is a critical character trait. It does not mean we need to be subservient or act like a slave, instead it means being courteously respectful of others. Humbleness is the character trait of not being proud or arrogant. It is the trait of valuing and respecting others (and it is difficult to find). It does not mean that we don't have an opinion or are a yes-man (or yes-woman). Norman Vincent Peale said, "Believe in yourself! Have faith in your abilities! Without a humble but reasonable confidence in your own powers you cannot be successful or happy."[38] **Humbleness includes being comfortable with ourselves and with the position we are going to play on the team.** It's about what we can quietly contribute to the success of the team and the organization.

Six. Build Trust

One of the intangibles that a Synergetic Follower creates is trust. The effort of building trust takes time and requires discipline. Trust can be built up over years, but can be lost in an instant. One of the best ways to build trust is to have integrity, which should be a common character trait, but, it seems to be missing in a lot of places. It is often missing in the workplace. **Essentially, integrity, is saying what you do and doing what you say.** It has more to do with understanding who we are and being consistent about it, so that others can trust in and depend on the commitments we make. Former Wyoming senator Alan Simpson said, "If you have integrity, nothing else matters. If you don't have integrity, nothing else matters."

Seven. Active Followership

Synergetic Followership doesn't occur by watching (or listening). We can't sit up in the bleachers observing—we have to get down on the field and be involved. Some people think that following is just doing what the leader asks and nothing more. Synergetic Followership actually anticipates requests that the leader has not asked for yet. This requires **active** following, including active listening and thinking when the leader delegates a task or project.

Eight. Managing Up

Too often we think that it's only important to manage down (i.e. manage those who report to you). However, good leaders count on a great follower to "manage up" (i.e. manage the leader) in order to help them be successful. There are a number of ways to do this including intervening in situations where the leader is about to make a bad decision and keeping the leader safe. It's the active process of managing the leader in a non-intrusive way. We need to always be managing up—true leaders depend on it.

Nine. Communicate and Handle Conflict

When we refer to communication, it includes written, digital and verbal skills. From text messaging to email to letters to formal documents and white papers, we need to be able to handle all of today's media well.

One of the tougher challenges to good communication is in situations where there is conflict. Too often people try to avoid conflict (except the few who love to create it). When it's unavoidable, there is often a desire to reduce conflict or halt it for a time. Being a Synergetic Follower means that conflict, when appropriate, should not be avoided. Instead, it should be dealt with head-on and resolved with professional, contextual, issue-related confrontation.

Ten. Make Decisions Based on Data

As we know, good leaders don't make all the decisions (thankfully). In fact, the really good leaders prefer to make fewer decisions and focus specifically on the strategic and policy decisions that need to be made to guide the organization, as well as a few critical decisions that only the person at the top can make. Excellent leaders count on having a lot of decisions made based on data and facts before they get to their level.

Now that we've briefly covered the 10 components to Synergetic Followership, we'll dig into each of them a little deeper.

Chapter 12
One. Believe in the Mission and the Leader

This is a foundational concept for a Synergetic Follower. **If we don't believe in the leader and the mission of the organization or company, then it will be very difficult to be successful as a Synergetic Follower.** Let's look first at the mission that we will be following. Peter Drucker, international consultant, author and the person who coined the term, "knowledge worker" said, "A mission cannot be impersonal; it has to have deep meaning, be something you believe in and something you know is right."[39]

If we don't buy-in to the mission of the organization that we are serving then we need to stop and rethink why we are here.

It is not uncommon for people to find themselves engaged in some effort, either in a job or as a volunteer or being part of a movement and never really think about why they are doing it. We need to ask ourselves, "Will this organization take us where we want to go in life?" Or let's even dial the time span down a bit, "Will it take us where we want to go in 5 years?"

So it's important to pause at this point, in the very beginning of our discussion, to ask if this is what we want to be involved in. Is this an organization and mission that we can believe in? Is this where we want to spend the next few years (or the rest of our life)?

Hopefully the leader we will choose or have chosen believes strongly in the mission of the organization, the work it does, and in driving that work forward. It will be difficult to follow the leader unless we have belief in the organization and mission as well.

Mission statements tend to be a little broader than slogans or taglines, which are designed to boil the mission down to just a few words. They tend to reflect the organization's current focus. The most famous is Nike's "Just do it." Let's take a look at some past slogans and taglines of other recognized organizations (this doesn't necessarily mean these companies have achieved their vision):

- 3M – "To solve unsolved problems innovatively"
- Mary Kay Cosmetics – "To give unlimited opportunity to women."
- Merck – "To preserve and improve human life."
- Wal-Mart – "To give ordinary folk the chance to buy the same thing as rich people."
- Walt Disney – "To make people happy."

So let's ask ourselves some questions about our own company or organization:

- What is the mission of the organization we're working or volunteering for?
- Do we understand it? What does it stand for?
- Does the organization still address the purpose identified in its mission statement?
- What has it accomplished in the past?
- What are the current slogans, goals and major projects?
- How engaged are we in working to accomplish the mission?

If we don't know the answers to these basic questions, that doesn't necessarily mean we're in the wrong place or following the wrong leader or organization. But it does mean that we will need to do some research and reflection on the organization we are following. **Once we know the mission and more about where the organization is going and what it**

stands for, we can make a choice to stay or leave—and begin our journey. If we can't find ourselves able to support the mission, we should start looking for another organization that matches our goals better. Making that decision is critical to being successful. Until then, we'll just continue to put in time.

If you don't agree or believe in the mission, then you'll begin to discover the negative ripple effect your lack of belief has on the work we do and how it causes conflicts during difficult projects and challenges. That brings us back to the main question—why are you working for an organization that you don't believe in? Start your exit plan now.

If you're not happy at your current workplace, you are not alone. A recent national poll by the Conference Board found that 55% of Americans are not satisfied with their work.[40] This is the lowest level since they started the poll 22 years ago. Just think what impact it would have if all of those people made a choice to find a place to work for that they could believe in and invest in.

Let's take an inventory of the attitudes of the followers around us. Is it a sweat-shop, do the people look sad, do they tend to look down a lot without much eye-contact? Or is this a company where the workers are upbeat and there is a sense of hope and energy about them and they believe that the work they are doing is significant.

So why do people stay in a job they don't like and don't believe in? Often they stay for the money or security that it provides, which is pretty low on Maslow's Hierarchy of Needs.[41] The motivation of the Synergetic Follower is on a higher level, because they are choosing where they work and who they work for.

There are some that say we don't have a choice of where we want to work or who we want to follow. We disagree, that choice is fundamental to who we are and what we want to become. This decision is one we should not give up on; it's one we should think hard about; it's one of the most important decisions we make in our career and life. **It requires that we have the courage to make a choice of who to follow.** Let's reflect more on the organization's mission:

1. Is it something that captures us?
2. Do we really believe in it?
3. Is it a mission and vision we can give ourselves to?
4. Are we willing to work towards that mission regardless of the obstacles that bureaucracy and bad leaders put in our way?
5. Are we willing to work extra, without pay sometimes, in order to help accomplish the mission?
6. Are we willing to work collaboratively with others for the success of the mission, even if they might not be that easy to work with?

If we believe in the mission of the organization, then let's look at the leader next. As we have said, we can tell a lot about the leader by looking at the followers. The types of followers in an organization are often a reflection of the type of leadership the organization has.

1. Are they enthusiastic about where the business or organization is going?
2. Are they energetic and have a sense of purpose in what they are doing?
3. Do they work in teams as a collaborative body or do we find a lot of individual efforts and an attitude towards helping others only when it is required?
4. Are they creative and innovative?

If the followers exhibit some, or all, of these characteristics, then that says a lot of about the leadership. No matter how wonderful and inspiring the mission is, if the leader is bad, the followers in the organization won't be happy about being there.

Let's look around the workplace. How do people work together and what are they like? Is this the right place for you to work?

If the business or organization is big enough, sometimes we can find a good leader to follow inside it, even if it's not a great company. If there is a good leader inside of an average organization, one of two things usually happens:

1. The good leader will be promoted often and will help change the average organization into a better one all along the way (stick close to this one).

2. The good leader leaves the average organization and takes one or more of his/her followers with them (which could be one of us).

So if we find ourselves inside an average organization with a mission that we minimally believe in, but we have a good or great leader, then we should stay put. Even if that leader is not in the top spot of the company or in the next circle of leaders, it's still better to stick with the good leader when you find one. This is especially true if the leader has been moving up in the organization over time and is gaining influence.

That doesn't mean that mission isn't still important, but, it's just as important for the Synergetic Follower to find a good leader.

As we've mentioned, there aren't really that many good or great leaders compared to the average or bad ones. Finding a good one can be even more difficult than finding a good organization. Talented leaders are involved at all levels in leading all types of organizations. In fact, many love the challenge of being involved in an average or below-average company and working with others to turn it into a great company. These are exciting leaders to follow and there is usually a lot of risk and challenge, but the result can be a transformed company or organization.

So if we're already working for a good or great leader, then we should stay with that person. If the leader leaves, there's a good chance they will take their best people with them—and we want the opportunity to be one of them (remember we still get to choose).

When we say "believe in the leader", that phrase probably needs a little more definition. Belief can range from "I believe that you are a decent person" all the way to, "I believe that your leadership is world-class and your wisdom is almost supernatural and I will follow you to the ends of the earth." The strength of our belief in the leader will have a direct impact on our success (and the leader's success).

However, this belief in the leader's vision, skills, and character needs to be based in reality, and not just blind following. It's important to remember that the leader is not perfect. At the beginning we might think that the leader is nearly perfect (we can be assured that they are not). Leaders, like the rest of us, learn from making mistakes and a leader who doesn't occasionally fail is someone who isn't taking enough risks.

But the impact of our belief in the leader is more powerful than we recognize. As John Stuart Mill, the acclaimed philosopher and political economist said, "One person with a belief is equal to ninety-nine who have only interests."

There are many slogans and sayings that remind us that we learn from our mistakes, not our successes. While this may be a little hard to believe, leaders often make more mistakes than others (sarcasm intended). It's important for us to expect that our leader will make mistakes and anticipate them whenever possible. Outstanding leaders are often able to admit those mistakes and apologize for them, learn from them and figure out a way to make amends or correct the situation.

Organizations and companies are not perfect either and they also make mistakes. The reality is that both leaders and organizations slip-up—we have to accept this. However, an organization or company that is not perfect and makes mistakes is not the same as a bad organization. A bad organization makes mistakes as well, but we're defining a bad organization as one that is "intentionally" being bad— it is selfish, doesn't take care of its staff, and may even be corrupt in some way. The bad organization is unhealthy and has leaders that are intentionally bad and their "mistakes" are on purpose.

The same goes for bad leaders. There's a big difference between a good leader who has flaws and a bad leader who also

has flaws. A bad leader is focused on themselves, misman-
ages people intentionally, and sometimes is corrupt. We need
to be realistic about leaders and organizations as we search
for a good leader to follow.

Side Note: Sometimes we are upset with a leader because we
think that some action on the leader's part that discounts us,
is actually intentional. For instance, we might take offense
at the leader because they did not invite us to an important
meeting or because they called someone else about a problem
that we were the most knowledgeable person to talk to about
it. In many cases these situations could just be mistakes. **We
need to allow the leader to make blunders occasionally
and not accuse them of doing something intentional when
it was just a mistake.** It doesn't happen often, but if we do
discover that the leader is intentionally discounting us and
it's not just a mistake or oversight, then we need to find a new
leader.

There is also a difference between authentic leadership and
"positional" leadership. We wouldn't want to encourage you
to follow someone who is only a positional leader. That is
someone who has the "title" or job position of a leader, but
doesn't lead. This is common in many organizations where
someone has been promoted beyond their capability to lead
or in a situation where someone has been given the leadership position and title because they are a friend or relative

of the boss. It can also happen out of desperation. For example, a position could have opened up and the positional-leadership-style person was the only applicant for it or the only person in line for the position.

We're talking about people who have leadership titles like manager, supervisor, or vice president, but they don't know how to lead. I'm sure we can think of several of those types of individuals without straining. Regardless of how they got into being a positional leader, these are the wrong types of leaders to choose to follow. If we follow too close to these types of leaders, then when executive management discovers that they aren't really leading and removes them, they may remove us as well thinking we contributed to the failure.

Sometimes the "real" leader that everyone is following, reports to and is a follower of a positional leader. This real leader has the wisdom, skills, and character that cause others to choose to follow them (including the positional leader sometimes). The real leader could be someone like an assistant, an engineer, or an analyst—the type of position doesn't really matter. This *real* leader leads from within the group and takes responsibility for the success of the group, even though the positional leader will usually get the public credit.

As we talk about different types of leaders, we encourage you to find the kind of leader that you can follow and learn from.

It will be difficult to find a leader that matches up with every-thing we've discussed (there aren't that many of them), but as long as they have several of the traits, skills, and knowledge that we've laid out, then you have increased your chances for success.

One thing to remember as we try to identify good leaders is that we don't really have to "like" the leader, although it can make things easier. Sometimes the best leaders are not neces-sarily charismatic or even likeable and may take some getting used to. If they are not enjoyable to be with, then we need to spend some time thinking about why we don't like them and if we will be able to get over what it is that bothers us (e.g. bad body odor, bad breath, doesn't smile much, annoying man-nerisms, etc.).

However, just because they aren't charismatic or friendly, doesn't make them a bad leader. In fact, Jim Collins in his book *Good to Great* says that the best long term leaders, ac-cording to his research, are usually not charismatic.[42]

Conversely, liking a leader at the beginning doesn't neces-sarily make them worth the investment. Sometimes a char-ismatic leader isn't a very good team builder or manager. Often, successful charismatic leaders will have a non-char-ismatic leader that reports to them who really runs the orga-nization/company.

We'll continue to repeat the importance of *choosing the leader* instead of the other way around (which is how the world often views it). Remember, we are the ones with the choice to follow a leader or not. Granted, this is usually preceded by the leader creating the opportunity to follow. In addition, leaders can certainly recruit us (but they still cannot force us to follow). We get to choose. **Find an organization or business with a mission you can believe in and leadership that you can follow.** This decision is critical for the Synergetic Follower, the leader and the future success of the organization.

Chapter 13
Two. Team Work

The next key component for Synergetic Followers is team work. Let's remind ourselves of the first part of the definition of the word synergetic, "*working together* in a creative, innovative, and productive manner." In past decades, projects and goals tended to be more focused on work that an individual did. Back when the assembly line actually had people on it (instead of robots), each individual had their own task to complete, whether it was welding a part of the car frame or attaching one of the wheels. Years ago, in sales, each person had their specific territory to cover and was measured based on individual results. This was a result of the industrial age. Before the industrial age, things were actually more collaborative. In the old family farm it took everyone in the family (and often extended family) to operate the farm.

However, in today's world the focus on the individual has gone the way of the assembly line. Working in our own silo is passé, today everything seems to be tied to a team. Vince Lombardi, the great Green Bay Packers coach, had it right when he said, "Individual commitment to a group effort—that is what makes a team work, a company work, a society work, a civilization work." This has been true of most sports for some time, but a team-orientation is now prevalent in business, nonprofit organizations, and in government and education. Even on the Internet, we have moved from Web 1.0, which was based on individuals visiting single entity websites to Web 2.0 and 3.0 which involve thousands or millions of individuals interacting and working with each other in a shared environment.

Many organizations understand this concept of working as a community. Jeffrey Pfeffer says, "Both longer-term employment and time horizons and the belief that senior leadership is concerned about employee welfare characterize more community-like companies."[43] As a result of this focus on team work, the style of leadership has changed as well. Leaders now carefully look at the knowledge, resources, experience, and skills of the different team members and how to combine those in order to achieve the results they are seeking. In some situations, if a team is lacking a particular skill or experience, someone who has it is located within another team and brought in to assist. **One thing is clear, having a team of people who work collaboratively together utilizing their strengths is much more effective than working with a group of individuals who are focused on their own personal contribution.**

Sports Team Examples

Almost any pro sports team has had a few years where the right combination of strengths and leadership resulted in winning the top trophies. That includes basketball teams like the Lakers or the Celtics, football teams like the Cowboys or the Packers, and baseball teams like the Yankees or the Giants. In business, that would include the team that created the first Macintosh or the first IBM PC, the Whiz Kids headed up by McNamara in the 50's, and the medical team of 20 surgeons headed up by Dr. Barnard, that did the first successful human heart transplant.

This concept of working in teams is very important. It changes the way we work with others and how we view the team we're involved with. We need to know how to be a selfless, contributing team member and provide the active engagement that is necessary for success.

The best teams have an excellent leader/coach and good followers who work collaboratively utilizing their diverse strengths (knowledge, skills, and resources) to accomplish the goal. They trust in the strengths of their teammates, relying on their diversity to solve difficult challenges, and know how to work together to bring out the best in the other team members. The legendary Notre Dame football coach, Knute Rockne said, "The secret is to work less as individuals and more as a team. As a coach, I play not my eleven best, but my best eleven." It's also important to have team members who are motivated to help the team succeed without needing to take credit for their individual contribution, but who promote the team's success.

Willingness to Do the Unpopular Jobs

Lots of people want to do the fun tasks, the easy things, the projects that have lots of glamour and excitement. In contrast, most leaders are looking for people who are willing to take on the tough projects or tasks, no matter how difficult or unpopular.

Part of being a Synergetic Follower is that we're willing to jump in and do the work that others won't do or are trying to avoid. Volunteering to take on work that others are trying to get out of is something that can be done even if we are not very skilled at the task. What's even better, a Synergetic Follower will enlist others to tackle the unpopular task. Leaders love to have someone on their team that is willing to roll up their sleeves and work on something that's dirty or repetitive or miserable (and they love to promote followers like that to better positions). It's important to note that a lot of leaders achieved their positions by doing the less attractive tasks along the way.

While leaders often get the credit for what gets done, we all know it's the people behind the leader who are doing the real work. It only took a few pharaohs to 'build' the Pyramids of Egypt, but in reality, it required 30,000 workers 23 years to build them. The Empire State Building involved 3,400 workers back in 1930 and over a year to complete. Both of these building projects are still standing.

The transistor, which powers every computer ever built was designed and created by a team of little-known scientists who worked for Bell Labs: John Bardeen, Walter Brattain and William Shockley[44] back in 1947 when vacuum tubes ruled the earth. It's encouraging to know that as a follower we can be involved in projects that change the world forever.

Chapter 14
Three. Seek Diversity of Strengths

This topic might have been able to be included in the section on teams, but it's important enough to stand alone. The two terms, Diversity and Strengths, are not usually associated with each other, so let's look at them separately first before we look at them as a single concept.

Strengths

The term "strength-based" has been around for a while and was popularized by Marcus Buckingham in his best-selling book, *Now, Discover Your Strengths.*"[45] One of the processes he describes that he said needs to be viewed differently is the work of evaluating staff in a business. Too often we point out the weaknesses that an employee has, instead of starting with their strengths (often an employee's strengths aren't even mentioned). Buckingham's research showed that an employee has to work long and hard to bring a "weakness" that they have up to a level that is mediocre at best. However, with the same level of effort, the employee can raise something that they do at a good level up to a great level.

Instead of focusing on weaknesses, this "strengths" approach can be used on a broader basis than just personnel evaluations. It has been utilized in communities for decades to revitalize neighborhoods according to authors John McKnight and Jody Kretzmann in their book, *Building Communities from the Inside Out*.[46] They now work for the Asset-based Community Development Institute at Northwestern University. Their strategy has been that instead of looking at the deficits or weaknesses in a neighborhood (e.g. poverty and crime), we should look at the assets or strengths (leaders, groups/associations, skills) in the neighborhood and build on and encourage them. This concept is very important for Synergetic Followers, especially as we tackle large problems and issues.

Major problems should be looked at from a strengths-based approach where, with the right diverse team, they can have a significant positive impact. We can look at each situation and instead of getting lost in all the challenges, we begin to look at what's working and what resources and assets (i.e. strengths) we have that will help us resolve it. This is a more positive approach and shows to our leader that we are pulling people and resources together and utilizing the assets that we have. It's much better than having the leader see us wringing our hands over the challenges. We'll find that if we work in this way that most leaders will want to keep us around.

Unpopular Strengths

Some strength surveys have asked people what their "gifts or talents" were. These surveys showed that most people believe that they have the gift or strength of leadership and management. But only a very few believe that they have the gift of "servanthood" or of "following." Yet when we look at the normal population, there aren't really a lot of leaders. This may be why many of the people around us may not volunteer or jump in on tasks that might be described as beneath a leader when there's work that needs to get done. People view those types of tasks as something a servant would do, not someone who should be a leader. This is our opportunity as a Synergetic Follower to jump in, tackle the project, and get it done.

Mike Rowe, star of the hit TV Show, *Dirty Jobs* where he looks at messy, gross and dirty jobs said, "It's surprising how many people come home from relatively 'clean' jobs at the end of the day feeling bitter and miserable. Whereas the people I meet, by and large, seem really content with their lives, and happy with their dirty jobs."[47] Half of the problem with undesirable projects is our attitude. If we would just get over the fact that no one wants to do these projects because they are so undesirable, we would be able to tackle them much quicker.

Diversity

Although a lot of people use the word "diversity," it is also a word that can get a lot of people upset. I've seen it used to beat up on homogenous groups, because they aren't "diverse" enough. In some cases diversity is also viewed as a weakness. When people are different, it can lead to misunderstandings, problems, fights, disagreement, and confrontations. Diversity is really about different thoughts, opinions, cultures, and background (the things that make the world interesting). Instead it is viewed by many in a negative way (all the "isms" including racism and classism). But if we look at diversity as a "positive" then we can see that having a diverse group or team has the potential to bring different ideas, approaches, and people together in creative and innovative ways that are very powerful. Malcom Forbes, the publisher of Forbes magazine, defined it well: "Diversity: the art of thinking independently together."

Research has shown that most difficult challenges require creative approaches and out-of-the-box thinking. It also indicates that homogenous groups don't do well with the most difficult challenges. These studies have shown that when a homogenous group tackles a difficult problem, they are able to quickly come to consensus on how to work on it. But then they tend to get stuck, because there isn't enough diversity in the group to come up with a new and different idea that might lead to a breakthrough in solving the problem.

On the other hand, diverse groups, with the same challenge took a lot longer to establish a leader and come to consensus on an approach to the problem, because there were so many diverse ideas of how to do it. In the beginning, the diverse group had difficulty understanding what the different members were trying to say. However, in the end, the diverse group was able to pull together to solve the problem, which the homogenous group failed to do. The diverse group surpassed the homogenous group because they had different ideas, innovative thinking and a variety of backgrounds and approaches.

It turns out that diversity lends itself to innovation and creativity. There is something about thinking with others who think differently than you do that leads to innovation. However, it doesn't happen as often, because it's a lot easier to gather a bunch of people together who all think alike—but we'll get very little true creativity.

Seek Diversity of Strengths

Now, let's combine these two terms, "strengths" and "diversity" into a goal to "seek diversity of strengths" in a team. A good example of this is to take a look at some of the top performing sports teams. The best football team is not necessarily the one that has the best quarterback. A successful football team requires good half-backs and wide-receivers to receive the ball and move it forward. It also requires an outstanding offensive front line that can prevent the other team from sacking the quarterback and that has the ability to open up a gap for the half-back to run through. On the other hand, a homogenous team of eleven quarterbacks, no matter how outstanding they were, would never be successful. A good team incorporates the diverse strengths of each player into different positions that result in a winning team.

For the Synergetic Follower, it means we need to gather diverse individuals and utilize their unique thinking, different approaches, and varied experience to address projects and solve difficult problems and issues. Using a strengths-based approach with a diverse group will help us accomplish an immense amount of work and solve issues while others are stuck at the starting gate still trying to figure out how to tackle the problem. We need to view different ideas as a good thing. We need diverse approaches instead of the familiar old ones that come from working with the same people as we always do.

111

A Synergetic Follower seeks and understands the power of a diversity of strengths on a team.

Chapter 15
Four. Just Do It

Nike made the phrase, "Just Do It" popular, calling on us to quit talking about it, analyzing it, wondering how it will be, and wondering if and when we should do it—and just do it. Seth Godin, one of my favorite authors, has a similar phrase, "Just Ship It." In his recent book, Linchpin, he says, "*The only purpose of starting is to finish,* and while the projects we do are never really finished, they must ship. Shipping means hitting the *publish* button on your blog, showing a presentation to the sales team, answering the phone, selling the muffins, sending out your references. Shipping is the collision between your work and the outside world."[48]

One component of the definition of the word synergetic is "productive." The Synergetic Follower understands these concepts of "Just Do It" and "Just Ship It"—and remains focused on being productive.

Leaders count on followers who can deliver

Leaders like followers that work hard, make them laugh, are organized, always show up to work on time, stay late or work on weekends and are willing to drop everything to tackle a project. But they *love* followers that get things done—who know how to deliver.

This ability to work with others to deliver on tasks and projects is critical to the success of the leader and the Synergetic Follower. Whatever else we may do, we must finish, complete, achieve, produce, close the book on, execute, attain, conclude, nail it, defeat, consummate, accomplish . . . you get the idea.

We can talk about how important the process is (and it is), we can talk about the need for team work, we can work towards a compelling vision, all the wonderful things we've learned and journal all of it for future generations. **But we have to get something done, complete the task or reach a milestone— or we're not really helping the leader or the business.** When we look around us, we should see goals reached, milestones achieved, projects completed, mission accomplished. We can't ever let the need to deliver get out of focus.

This push for getting things done, doesn't mean that all the meetings, documents to read, bureaucracy, obstacles, failures and other processes along the way aren't necessary. In many cases these things are critical for success, but success is still the ultimate goal that needs to be achieved. If you're trying to get those processes under control, David Allen wrote a wonderful book designed to help, *Getting Things Done*[49] (or GTD for all those who follow his principles).

Setting expectations

One of the most important things we can do is to set expectations accurately. When we say something will be done on June15, then it needs to be done on June 15—not on June 16 at 2am or June 17 or July. It needs to be done on June 15. We should not commit to a date or time that we can't meet, even if that means disappointing the leader who wants something sooner. It's important to build trust (we'll talk more about that in a little bit) and a big component of building that trust is built on a track record that we can deliver when we say we can.

We chuckle when we read the quote from Douglas Adams, the author of *Hitchhiker's Guide to the Galaxy*, "I love deadlines. I like the whooshing sound they make as they fly by."

The setting of expectations is critical in our ability to deliver on time. However, missing deadlines has a lot to do with not setting the right expectations for the original deadline at the beginning.

We have to manage expectations or success will continually elude us. There are some lower-priority projects that we can push the timeline to deliver out further than required before we set expectations. This will open up time for other unanticipated projects that suddenly appear or allow us to deliver a little early on others. But we still need to deliver on the lower-priority project on the date that we commit to.

Side Note: If adjustments to the expectations are absolutely required, then make sure the leader is aware of those adjustments.

The setting of expectations for high priority projects is very important, because we have to make the deadline date. On the other hand, if we are too conservative with setting the expectations for delivery of a high-priority project, then the leader may look for someone else who will tackle the project more aggressively. The oft-used saying, "under-promise and over-deliver" is true because making the date is so important. However, if we constantly under-promise and deliver ahead of schedule then people will recognize that quickly and always expect us to deliver early. Deliver on time, and if you make a mistake on setting expectations, then err on delivering early—but only by a little bit.

No excuses

There will be times when expectations are missed and people are disappointed, including the leader. The Synergetic Follower resists the temptation to make excuses or blame others. This sounds easy—but when people are disappointed and they are looking for the cause and all eyes turn toward you, it is very difficult not to go down the excuse or blame path.

When we miss a deadline, we need to analyze and document what happened in an objective manner (at least for our own records), learn from our mistakes, grow stronger, adjust our setting of expectations in the future—but don't make up excuses or blame others.

Chapter 16
Five. Don't Seek Credit

The Synergetic Follower does not seek or claim credit for the accomplishments of the team. In the world of Donald Trump and Simon Cowell, being humble and not seeking credit doesn't seem to be as popular as it once was. However, it is one of the keys to success as a follower and to getting things done within a team. There seem to be a lot of misconceptions around those who are humble and don't seek credit. We're not using the term "humbleness" here to mean meek or wimpy. It's a way of doing work and letting the work stand for itself. The Synergetic Follower resists the temptation to spike the ball in the end zone.

When we avoid taking credit, we will find that it makes it easier for others to work alongside us and they'll enjoy it more. Think about how irritating it is if you are working with someone and every time your group accomplishes something that person takes the limelight and the credit for it. When that happens, the next time we have the opportunity to work with that individual, we will figure out a way not to work with them. When people take personal credit for a group effort it undermines morale and future productivity of the group. As Synergetic Followers, if the limelight falls on us too often, then it's probably a good indicator that we are taking too much credit and headed for trouble with the rest of the team.

Trying to avoid taking credit and remaining humble is a difficult task. Even if we are successful at that, people will still give us credit in many situations. Avoiding the "taking credit" opportunities that arise is not as easy as it sounds. We are actually culturally-raised to take credit when we've done something good—breaking that habit is difficult. Now that doesn't mean that we must do everything anonymously. It's just that we are understated about our work and that we try to do our work without attracting attention. We don't need to shine the light on ourselves. Leaders and those around us know who is doing good work.

One of the ways we can do this is to look for opportunities that don't have a lot of visibility, but are key to the success of the project or organization. These opportunities are all around us since no one else wants to volunteer for the undesirable work. People tend to work on things that are in the limelight, popular, fun or easy. We'll find lots of opportunity to do those things that aren't the first pick by everyone else. It only seems fitting that the undesirable work often ends up being more important than some of the fun stuff. When they build a house, laying the foundation looks pretty boring, but it's the reason the house can stand. Often if the "boring" work doesn't get done, then the whole project will fail.

The Synergetic Follower recognizes that the level of skills and capabilities and knowledge required for some of these invisible tasks may not be high, but they are often the most important work we can do. Astute leaders recognize the importance of invisible work as identified by Meyerson and Fletcher, "For senior managers who saw the link between the invisible work and theirs of moving to a team-based structure, the challenge was to find ways to make the invisible work visible."[50]

There are also great opportunities that come up when we work on projects or tasks that are less visible. But if we roll up our sleeves and get into this "less visible" work we will find a world of opportunities. Like the undesirable tasks we just discussed, it's often this type of work that makes the difference in a project's success or failure.

One misconception is that someone who doesn't seek credit and is humble has low self-esteem and that people who are proud have high self-esteem. There is actually no connection to these two. In many cases, a truly humble person often has high self-esteem and the proud individual has low-self-esteem. Having a healthy self-esteem and self-awareness means that we are confident in who we are and don't need to prove anything to others. Ben Franklin said, "To be humble to superiors is duty, to equals courtesy, to inferiors nobleness."

Self-awareness means that we have a good understanding of what our talents, skills, gifts, knowledge and experience are and how they can contribute to the success of the goals and projects that we are involved in. Most people think they are self-aware, but in reality they really don't know themselves very well. Although we assume that most people are self-aware, psychologist Mark Leary says, "People do not purposefully control their behavior in ways that are consistent with their attitudes, values and goals unless they are self-focused and monitoring themselves. Self-control requires self-awareness."[51]

When we find someone who is authentically **not** seeking to take credit, it is usually an indicator that they are humble.

An individual who is truly humble recognizes that they have talents and skills and experience, but so do others. In addition (key point coming), theirs aren't worth more or less than anyone else's. That does not mean that our contributions do not have value. We want to be part of a productive team, hopefully a diverse team where everyone contributes and is valued. We may feel that our skills are unique, but success in an organization and in helping a leader requires more than uniqueness these days. Success is rarely based on the efforts of one individual; it is usually a group or team effort that is the most successful. The best organizations have teams of "unique and diverse" people who work together collaboratively.

The skills, talents, character, and experience that we have are unique, but humble followers realize that everyone has unique skills and might be able to contribute to the success of a project and that there is no need to take individual credit for the contributions.

Unfortunately, some organizations value certain skills over others depending on their mission, products and services, which can lead to a difference in pay. For example at Microsoft, the person who writes great computer programs is highly valued, but at a small food market, that same person, even though they might be an incredible programmer, won't be valued for those skills at all.

The Synergetic Follower realizes that value is contextual.
In this organization, at this specific time in history, in this particular situation, one person may be more valuable to the project, goal, or company than another. A perfect example of this is Warren Buffet, the third richest person in the world, who has often said that he was lucky to be born in America and at the particular time he was born. Anywhere else and at any other time, he says he would not have been nearly as successful—it's what he calls the lottery of birth.

This ability to not seek credit is also important in leadership, as Jim Collins, author of *Good to Great*, says about the best leaders, "A Level 5 leader—an individual who blends extreme personal humility with intense professional will."[52]

There are a number of advantages to being someone who is humble and doesn't seek credit. Let's take a look at a few of those. On the positive side, three of the advantages are:

1. People like to work with someone who is humble and doesn't seek credit all the time. There is great benefit and enjoyment in working with somebody who is not prideful or arrogant and isn't always talking about themselves. A lot of people really don't care for a person who takes credit for everything. They tend to ignore them and steer away from them when it comes to working on a team. We tend to like humble people

who don't need to bask in the glow of their own accomplishments. It's nice to know that when we talk to a humble person we don't have to listen to the long litany of things they have done in the past and we won't have to hear about how great they are or all the people they know. People seek out the opportunity to work with someone who is talented, but humble.

2. Another advantage to being self-aware and humble is that it lowers the pressure that others might put on us. It helps set realistic expectations of what expectations of us should be. The prideful and arrogant person often sets expectations much higher than they can deliver—and then blames others when they aren't successful. Humbleness, self-awareness, and self-esteem all contribute to an attitude that says this is what I can do well and this is what I'm not good at. By identifying what our strengths and weaknesses are, it allows us to fit into the team appropriately.

3. A third advantage is that there is learning and growth that comes from being humble, because it is not a natural way of operating for most people. For some historical or cultural reason it appears that there is a natural tendency to promote ourselves and talk about how good we are. The TV hit show, American Idol, is focused on finding the next big star—but with

thousands of applicants, there is still only one winner. Being humble and not seeking credit is not a natural trait for most people and is rarely encouraged by the media or those around us. It requires effort and time to develop this type of attitude. But it's worth it and there is a lot of positive growth and learning that comes as a result.

Over time, the humble follower will quietly find a way into the best positions that have the most growth and the most opportunities.

If we're new to this idea of not-seeking-credit and being humble and it seems impossible to do, then start by "pretending" to be humble. Since being humble is not natural, it will seem a little strange in the beginning, but over time it will become real as we see how it works. If we stay at it, eventually our humbleness will become real. There is a lot of strength in someone who is truly humble— their work speaks much louder than their words.

There are many ways to work towards this attitude. One thing we can do is cut down on the use of the word "I," as in "I did this" or "I'm going here" or "I think this" or "I feel this." By changing our vocabulary, it also has an impact on our thoughts and actions. Instead, if we'll talk about the team, the leader, the organization or anything except our own importance, it will literally change the way we perceive ourselves and the way the world sees us.

Chapter 17
Six. Build Trust

Building trust is one of the most important efforts of a Synergetic Follower. Stephen Covey opens up his book, *Speed of Trust* with, "Trust impacts us 24/7, 365 days a year. It undergirds and affects the quality of every relationship, every communication, every work project, every business venture, every effort in which we are engaged. It changes the quality of every present moment and alters the trajectory and outcome of every future moment of our lives—both personally and professionally."[53]

Trust is something that takes time to develop, but once the team has trust among the members—tasks and projects can move much faster. Trust is something that starts with one person, but someone has to take that first step to trust another. However, we usually take that step of faith with someone who we "believe" will be trustworthy and have integrity. We put quotes around "believe" because trust is not an intellectual exercise, it is a step of faith—it takes action to prove that it exists.

The Synergetic Follower builds trust by taking that that step of faith and trusting the teammates that he/she can trust (or at least appear to be trustworthy). But it also requires that we work hard at being trustworthy and having integrity.

Although the term "integrity" is highly valued in the workplace, it is actually a scarce trait in many organizations and is often only given lip service. The Synergetic Follower can change that and help develop an organization that has integrity, where people and processes can be trusted.

We've defined integrity as, "saying what we are going to do and doing what we say." In their book on Southwest Airlines, Kevin Freiberg and Jackie Freiberg say, "Integrity means doing what you say you are going to do and being the person you are. Integrity gives you trust and credibility, without which you can have no influence."[54] When we say, "doing what you say" it doesn't necessarily mean that you are doing things "right"—that's a whole different discussion. However, there should be integrity in all that we say and how we act and operate, which then makes us very dependable, credible and trustworthy. Leaders and colleagues can trust that we are going to act in a certain way, that is, if we say we're going to do something then we'll do it.

Some of the confusion around the term "integrity" is because there is a difference between internal integrity and external integrity. Internal integrity is related to our own internal conversations with ourselves. This is a process that allows us to justify almost everything we do and still keep our internal integrity. For instance, we might be able to justify the need to run through a stop sign because we're really late and there are no other cars, and it's safe (or at least appears to be).

Another example is the thought that it is all right to borrow (forever) that calculator from our workplace without telling anyone so that we can use it at home. We might accomplish justification by reasoning that it will be easier and cheaper for the organization to have us take the calculator then to purchase it with our own money and go through all the trouble of justifying it and having the organization reimburse the money to us. But if we don't ask or tell anyone about it, then regardless of what we think, it's considered stealing by companies and organizations.

Both of those are examples of how we might justify "internally" what we do. Studies confirm this by showing that 17 percent of people in the country run stop signs, and 58% of people speed in sections where the speed is posted. In other words, a lot of us are "internally" justifying doing things against the rules.

Now for a couple examples that don't violate traffic or theft laws. Let's say we're going to include three potential clients in our sales contact list in our Friday report because we need to make our sales report look better. However, we didn't actually contact those three clients, but we're planning to see them on Monday, and no one will really notice that we didn't visit them last week. While this may be legal, it still violates our integrity. As the saying goes, "Just because we can do it, doesn't mean we should." The sales report will not be an accurate reflection of what really happened. In other words, "what we said we would do, is not what we did."

Let's look at one more example—when the leader asks us to do something that we consider meaningless and a waste of time (we have all been in situations like this). We know our leader is likely to forget that they asked us to do it by tomorrow, so we'll respond by telling them that we'll take care of it. However, we then ignore the request, counting on the leader's track record of forgetting the request within 24 hours. This allows us to continue working on what we perceive to be the more important tasks that our leader assigned last week. We're sure that they would rather have us work on those instead of this new one that seems like a waste of time. Basically, it's easier to say that we'll do it knowing that it will be forgotten later on, instead of pushing back and saying why we shouldn't do it. Internal integrity is simple to do because we are abiding by our own rules instead of external rules. The problem is that internal integrity often conflicts with external integrity—this conflict can destroy our credibility and trustworthiness.

Going back to our base rule, integrity is about doing what we say. What laws, rules, or faith we believe in, is not the topic here—it's our actions. Let's return to our example of the sales report. If we maintain our integrity, then we won't falsely add the extra three clients to the list and we'll let the leader know that we will make it up next week. The leader is going to be a little disappointed that the report is short of their expectations, but they will know that in the future when we have a problem finishing a task, they can count on us to approach them and talk about it.

Let's take a look at a situation where our integrity might be challenged in a different way. For instance, the leader asks us to do something technically legal, but against the moral code that we believe in. How do we handle that? These are more difficult situations, where what to do and what not to do isn't as clear. Or what about when the leader asks us to do something outside of our job description or even something inappropriate like picking up the leader's clothes at the dry cleaners. How far outside of the job description do we go— what's really inappropriate? Who is right? The problem can also be related to the perception of the request. Sometimes the leader will ask us to do something that the leader feels is completely in line with our job description, but we don't agree. So there's a discrepancy in perception and how we deal with those types of situations are important for growth for both the follower and the leader.

In a final example, let's say the leader makes a mistake that costs the company money, but the leader doesn't say anything and no one knows about it, except for us. Do we say anything about it or do we "follow" the leader's example and say nothing? This has more to do the leader's lack of integrity, which then challenges the follower's integrity. There is a book by Ira Chaleff called, *The Courageous Follower: Standing Up To & For Our Leaders*[55] that really covers these situations well, where the leader does something that isn't right and involves the follower (or the follower is aware of it).

What's the right thing to do? The easy answer is to do what you think is right. However some of these situations are so complex that the "right thing" to do is difficult to perceive. That is the difficulty with integrity, there are so many situations that have all kinds of circumstances that we can't answer these issues definitively without all of the context. It takes wisdom, experience and maturity to make the right decision. Mistakes will be made, but the important thing is that we will learn from them and move forward. It's still about learning to do what we say and say what we do. Recognizing that people make mistakes and fail all the time on their path to maturity, this is a key lesson for the Synergetic Follower.

In all of these situations, it's important for us to match up the internal and external integrity and understand that often the "perception" of events is only the truth as we see it (and that others may "perceive" it differently). The leader needs to know that we are going to do what we say and if we are unable to do that, we will tell them. Integrity is not as easy as we think, since there are shades of grey that are created by different perceptions. But it is critical that we have integrity. As Warren Buffet has said, "In looking for people to hire, you look for three qualities: integrity, intelligence, and energy. And if they don't have the first, the other two will kill you."

Chapter 18
Seven. Active Followership

Although we've already said this several times, let's just make the foundational statement again, "all leaders need good followers." However, sometimes leaders don't get the type of people that they really need or are looking for. And some followers don't give the right kind of help. And in some cases, the followers might want to be helpful, but they just don't know how to do it.

Active Following

There are a lot of ways to divide up the different types of followers. Let's look at one way—active versus passive. Passive followers are the ones that we read and hear about the most.

The media depicts them as blindly following the leader. They are often pictured and referred to as lemmings and are described as being yes-men and yes-women who agree with the leader no matter how dumb an idea it is.

Mohandas Gandhi said, "A 'No' uttered from the deepest conviction is better than a 'Yes' merely uttered to please, or worse, to avoid trouble." Passive followers don't have much of a spine and prefer not to confront anyone or do anything risky. They are usually quiet and tend to just react to whatever the leader wants and are rarely proactive about projects and tasks. They see themselves as just another of the workers who shouldn't have an opinion or even an original idea. There's nothing outstanding about what they do and they don't stand-out in the crowd in any way. In fact, for many of them, their goal is to fade into the background—it's less risky if no one sees you or knows about you. They tend to be nameless and make up a large part of the organization. They can be good workers, but they're not the kind of followers we are talking about in this book.

Groupies are another form of passive followers. They are focused on the leader, not the organization, or company. They also follow blindly and without thinking. However, they are a little bit more energetic than the typical passive follower and their focus on the needs of the leader and treating them like a rock star is their signature.

135

Active followers, on the other hand, are fewer in numbers compared to the passive ones. They are engaged and focused in over-delivering on the effort the leader is looking for. Focus and action are their keys to success, as Alexander Graham Bell said, "Concentrate all your thoughts upon the work at hand. The sun's rays do not burn until brought to a focus." Active followers are different than groupies, who are very engaged and active but still do exactly what the leader says. Active followers are more than that—we don't always agree with the leader, we are creative and think ahead, we make things happen and we get things done.

We also pull people together. We are perfect team members and are willing to lead when it is appropriate and necessary. Another benefit is that we require very little management by the leader. The best Synergetic Followers are low-maintenance.

One of the key actions that the active follower does is to pull people together because success often depends on teams. They help create teams, even though they might not be the leader of it. The ability to recruit others into the team or organization is one of big assets of an active follower.

Another key trait is thinking ahead. Instead of waiting for instructions, the active follower is thinking about the mission, and goals and what the leader is thinking. The active follower anticipates what will be needed, so that by the time the leader is ready, they have already started laying the foundation for the work ahead.

As Synergetic Followers, we are not just active followers, we are also always thinking ahead. We have made the choice to follow, so let's do it in an active way. An active follower provides an incredible service to the leader and organization.

Don't Do the Minimum

Winston Churchill said, "I am easily satisfied with the very best." Unfortunately, there are a lot of followers who are interested in doing the very minimum amount of work that is required. In many government jobs, where being fired is rare, doing the minimum required seems to be an art form. Synergetic Followers don't care what the minimum requirements are, because they are so engaged and focused in excelling and over-delivering that it's not even a concern. Another advantage for the leader is that they can leave us to our work and it will get done. There is also more of a two-way relationship that develops between the leader and the active follower. The leader begins to depend on us for feedback, input and ideas. The relationship grows and becomes far more than just the leader giving assignments and the follower completing them.

Getting Started

So let's talk about how we can be more active in our follower-ship. It may seem obvious, but the first step is to "make the decision" to step down from the bleachers and onto the field. It's time to stop watching from the stands and start actively changing our world. It will involve effort, sacrifice, perhaps embarrassment—but we can't be a Synergetic Follower until we take this step.

When we take this step, it's usually best not to tell the leader. Most leaders don't know what to do with someone who says, "I want to follow you." It can almost sound like a stalker—so let's not talk about it, just do it (more on that later). There are several components to being a more active follower, including the following:

1. **Do research.** Do the research to find out what the best options for challenging issues/projects are and what kinds of decisions the leader has made in the past in those situations.

2. **Anticipate.** This is one of the defining traits of those who have chosen to be a Synergetic Follower. It's not something people are born with—it is a skill that is developed. In the book, *Implementation: making things happen* by Anita M. Pankake, she says, "Skills in anticipating and predicting all kinds of things—behavior, feelings, results, resource needs, conse-

quences and so forth—are important for facilitating
the coordination and collaboration of tasks."[56] Think
ahead and think beyond the task at hand. What is
the leader or organization going to need next? What
should we do to prepare? Anticipate.

3. **Mission.** Review the mission and big goals of the organization and keep it in mind all the time. What still
needs to be done in order to achieve those goals? Zig
Ziglar says, "I don't care how much power, brilliance
or energy you have, if you don't harness it and focus it
on a specific target, and hold it there you're never going to accomplish as much as your ability warrants."
Is the current work helping to accomplish the mission? If not, what can we do to move the agenda forward? So much wasted time and resources is spent on
tasks and projects that are not related to the mission.

4. **Opportunities.** Most people miss opportunities for
success because they aren't looking for them. Pay attention and look for opportunities that we can take
advantage of to help the organization and the leader.
Windows of opportunities open all the time and the
Synergetic Follower sees those opportunities and
takes advantage of them when they come. If we constantly procrastinate and just react to situations, we'll
rarely be able to anticipate or see opportunities—they
will just pass us by.

5. **Effort.** Success requires work—hard work. In the book about the need for hard work, *Hard Work: Success Made Easy* by Michael Crews and Ed Sweet, they say, "It's a circle of hard work and trust that's the engine for building successful teams and successful businesses."[57] It's important to work hard to make sure the organization and the leader achieve the goals and the mission. We need to put in more effort than the minimum and work to over-deliver on expectations. However, this by itself is not enough—there are a lot of hard workers that are needed. **What is needed is hard work combined with skills, creativity, innovation, and teamwork.**

6. **Document.** The Synergetic Follower knows the importance of documentation, which is something most of us don't want to do. Document, track, and monitor the work so that the results are captured. It won't take long for the leader to notice and want us involved in the most important projects. It's valuable because often the only way we can move forward is to have results and indicators that what we're doing is going to be successful. It's important to monitor success and failure, so we can adapt and modify what we are doing in order to stay on track for success. So one of the keys to future success is to take that extra time now to document, track, and monitor.

Followers Who Don't Help

We've already established the fact that leaders need followers, but often leaders don't get the followers they need. One of the keys to successful leadership is finding and recruiting the right team, which we'll talk about later. It means finding the right people, recruiting them to join the organization, and placing them in the right position. Excellent leaders, in order to be successful, spend a lot of time making sure they hire and gather the right staff around them. Unfortunately, followers don't always provide the right type of help (or their help is rather average). In some cases they may be trying to help, but they don't have the right strengths or skill or experience that is necessary for the task at hand. A person in the wrong position can sometimes pull things down no matter how well intentioned they are. The Synergetic Follower is sensitive to the needs of the leader and the organization, they look for opportunities to help, and actively take advantage of those opportunities to assist with accomplishing the mission.

Chapter 19
Eight. Managing Up

What is "Managing Up?" Actually it's a form of leadership upside-down. In addition to the goals and tasks that we are working on as followers, we are also responsible for managing our leader. Of course, this doesn't mean that the leader reports to us or has to do what we say (wouldn't that be nice). But don't be afraid to engage in managing up. Outstanding leaders not only know that the best followers manage up, they count on it.

Managing up requires subtle coaching and guiding without swapping roles. We are obviously not in charge, but it demands that we are involved in helping the leader become more successful. In some cases we are analyzing what is going on at the frontlines, almost like being a scout. We "scout" out ahead, we see what's going on, and we report what we find back to the leader. It helps the leader and provides eyes and ears to what's going on. Eric Bloom in his book on managers says, "Effective managing up is about communication, trust, standing your ground when needed, producing quality work, and being responsive to all levels of management."[58] This means producing results, building a team, and staying enthusiastic—and no whining.

The best leaders hire people that they know will manage up, subtly coach them, and help them be better leaders. **Good leaders know they don't have all the wisdom and knowledge, so finding followers, who complement their own strengths, is a top priority.**

The major problem is that most followers don't realize good leaders expect this of the staff who report to them. People often think that being a good follower is all about keeping the head down, focusing on the task at hand, and not making any trouble. Many followers believe that it is completely up to the leader to have all the vision, to look ahead and to tell them what to do.

Synergetic Followers are engaged in the work of today, but they are also looking ahead—and looking around. Dr. Brett Simmons, organizational behavior consultant says, "...we have a very hard time with the notion that in right relationship, it is just as much the follower's responsibility to help the leader transform."[59]

The first step to managing up is that the leader has to trust us—trust that we'll get our assigned work done and getting it done on time. If we come to the leader with new ideas, but we aren't getting our projects completed, then why would the leader pay much attention? The work accomplished as a follower has to be done well, and the leader has to count on that. When the base level of work is being accomplished, then we earn the right to influence and help the leader.

Machiavelli said, "A return to first principles in a republic is sometimes caused by the simple virtues of one man. His good example has such an influence that the good men strive to imitate him, and the wicked are ashamed to lead a life so contrary to his example."[60] Although we may not think that anyone is watching or paying attention to what we say and do—they are. We must be seen as someone who is thoughtful, thinks ahead, and gets things done.

There are a number of opportunities when we can manage up. For example, if the leader requests us to do something that will actually hurt the organization or take it in the wrong direction, then we have an opportunity to help our leader see that. Now comes the difficult part, how do we help the leader re-think the request without being insubordinate? We could ask the leader to help us understand or clarify the request. Often, when a leader has a chance to review a request with someone else, they will see that it doesn't make sense and doesn't move the business forward.

Balance in these types of situations is important. If we ask the leader to clarify the requests too often, then we become a nuisance, someone who has to have everything explained. But if our requests for clarification don't happen very often and when they do they result in the leader seeing that the request should be taken back or modified—then we're truly managing up.

Sometimes it takes more than a request for clarification for the leader to see that the request is wrong and we have to push back or challenge the leader to rethink what they are requesting or doing. When we say, "challenge the leader," this doesn't mean that we confront them in public or front of other colleagues. It means that we have to figure out how to say "no" politely, thoughtfully and in private. And if the leader disagrees with our recommendation and wants to make the decision anyway, then we will move forward with it unless it causes us to compromise in a way that we can't accept.

The leader has to gain trust that we will, as a follower, privately confront bad decisions (in an appropriate way) that the leader has made. If they have made a mistake with a request or a bad decision that will impact the organization then we should have the ability to pull them aside and tell them. And the leader has to have confidence that we are not trying to undermine them, but that we are sincerely trying to help.

Good leaders aren't threatened by followers who challenge them or provide feedback. In fact they are trained to look for or build in feedback from those that report to them. For example, in her book, *Motivate Like a CEO*, Suzanne Bates encourages the leader to build in a feedback loop, "When you encourage people to share bad news, your feedback loop is really working; you create a culture of people who are less afraid to take risks or report mistakes. People will be innovative or try an approach and share the results, good or bad, if they know that they won't get in trouble for trying and failing."[61] Good leaders count on feedback to help guide them and learn from their decisions.

If we have the type of leader that can't take any kind of pushback or challenge from us, then that's a bad sign. If they don't change or realize how it is helping them, eventually they will fail (it's not a pretty thing to watch).

Providing Options

It is rare that projects are successful without some obstacles or problems along the way. While the job of the follower is to resolve those problems, sometimes it requires direction from the leader to move forward. In those situations, it's important to provide the leader with options. There are few things more irritating to a talented leader than having a follower come in with a problem without doing enough research to provide some options for resolution. Or even worse, saying that the problem can't be solved. This requires the leader to stop what they are doing and identify the options to resolve the problem and look at potential results. They will also need to evaluate any collateral damage and other impacts and then make the decision. At some point, they will begin to wonder why they are doing our job and start to look around for someone to replace us.

Leaders count on us to research the problem and identify possible solutions and outcomes before coming to them. While it is rare, in some situations all of the options lead to bad outcomes. We still need to identify and define the options and figure out which of the options are the best of the bad choices (or the least of worst).

It is also helpful to clear the obstacles in the way of success whenever possible so that the best path is clearer. If we're doing our job as a follower correctly, it makes the leader's job easier. The leader can look and see more clearly what some of the options are and identify the best path.

Although tradition often points to the leader as the one who makes the decision, the reality is that everyone contributes to decision-making. **It is important that we make the decisions that are at our level, especially if it's not necessary for the leader to make it.** The higher the level of the decisions, the grayer and more difficult they are.

The easier choices should be done at the lower levels of the organization. Great leaders push decision-making down as far as it is appropriate. That means the most strategic and difficult decisions are made at the top and the easier (or clearer) decisions are made nearer to the front lines. Hanz Finzel in his book on leadership tells leaders, "The one who does the job should decide how it is done. The best management practice is to push decisions down to the people on the front lines. Let the people who are responsible for the outcome have as much ownership as possible in decision-making."[62]

I remember a colleague who was so afraid of doing something wrong that he would call his leader several times a day to check if he was making the right decision. As a result, he was moved to a different position after a year of these requests.

As a follower, if we push all the decisions up to the leader, then we reduce the time that the leader has to think strategically. The leader will not be able to look out to the future, because they are spending all of their time making tactical decisions.

For the decisions that are appropriate for us to make, we need to think about how the leader views the different choices or scenarios in the decision, what choice they will likely make and then make the decision. Don't take on decision-making that really should be made by the leader—or it can look like we're trying to take over the leader's responsibilities.

Good leaders trust us to make those types of decisions and push decision-making down to the lowest layers in the organization that is appropriate. It's important to document the research and other aspects of the decision so that others can go back to the information for reference and learn from our successes and failures.

Our managing up needs to be subtle and respectful. Over time it will develop into a positive relationship between the leader and the Synergetic Follower.

Chapter 20
Nine. Communicate and Handle Conflict

Two related capabilities that are necessary for the Synergetic Follower to have are communication skills and the ability to handle conflict. We've already discussed one of the communication skills that is important to have, which is managing up. There are many other types of communication that we need to be able to utilize.

We should capture the work that is going on so that it can benefit our leaders and our colleagues. We should provide regular status reports on projects or tasks or updates, even if the reports seem to be ignored (they won't be). These updates could be something as simple as an email.

150

Regular status reports based on data really operate like drip irrigation—and over time have a significant impact. The short update or status report is a way of speaking about the work without shining the light on ourselves. By keeping others informed factually, it will help them speak to the effort when the opportunity arises. In some situations, we might be the only one documenting the work. At the end, everyone will be thankful that someone was capturing the work of the team.

In addition, it is important to have good peer-to-peer communications. The Synergetic Follower has the ability to work well with colleagues and others on a team. That includes crossing normal boundaries and working with others from different teams, departments or with people from other organizations. In particular, boundary crossing is one of the keys to success—it's another example of "seeking diversity of strengths." **This type of communication requires that we are selfless in order to engage across boundaries.**

People are reluctant to work with those that they don't know well. Very few people like to work with strangers because they are often so . . . strange. A common reaction to being approached by a stranger is, "what do they want from me." By approaching others that we don't know well (or at all) in a way that looks for an opportunity of success for both of us, can eventually build a trust that will be the foundation of a successful team. This win-win approach is very effective when working across boundaries, as well as with colleagues on our own team.

Communication skills are critical in order to effectively communicate the mission, goals and projects of the organization. While this book can only touch on the importance of communication, there are literally thousands of books on developing communication skills and millions of websites on communication development. That's because it's a skill, not something we're born with. It's far more than just talking and listening. As Peter Drucker has said, "The most important thing in communication is hearing what isn't said." Good communication takes time to develop and the reason that there are so many books, classes and webinars on communication is because people aren't very good at it.

We've talked about communicating up to our leader and communicating with our peers and our colleagues. We've also talked about communicating with people that are in other departments or organizations and we've talked about working in teams. What about those followers who have staff reporting to them? Let's discuss a situation where as both follower and leader, we are working with frontline staff who report to us, influenced by us or temporarily assigned to us.

For Synergetic Followers who have the ability to work with frontline staff that report to them, it is important to understand how to lead while following. While this is really a type of leadership, it can be done with a style that matches and fits a follower.

A key concept in this "follower-style" of leadership is to listen often and listen well. This is very helpful when working with staff and direct reports. There are all kinds of information, ideas and wisdom that will be provided if we will just listen. This information, when aggregated and put together by us and provided to the leader, will help the leader and business move forward. In some cases it provides insight into a difficult problem that can now be resolved or saves the organization from making a major mistake.

It bears repeating what all the communication books and presentations say, "that it all starts with listening." Most of us tend to think that we listen well, but the reality is that we spend much of the time that someone else is talking preparing for our brilliant response. We don't really listen at all, except to listen for the next break in the flow of words so that we can jump into it with our opinion. It's important for us to set our potentially dazzling response aside for a few moments and really listen to what the other person is saying without planning what we're going to say in response.

Another important area of communication is with the company's customers or organization's constituents. The information that can be learned from customers is critical to an organization's success, but the customers are often ignored—someone needs to listen to them. Too often people discount what the customer says or interpret what they are communicating incorrectly. Failing to listen to the customer and others is the best path to failure. In the book, *Listening in everyday life: a personal and professional approach*, the authors talk about the impact of not listening when rolling out an initiative to improve service to the customer, "Service initiatives often fail because the effort improves service in ways the customer doesn't really care about—the organization hasn't listened."[63]

The best followers listen carefully to what the customer or constituent is saying and summarizes that information and includes implications and recommendations before forwarding to the leader.

Finally, being able to communicate with the public is important. The "'public" refers to people that are not customers, but their opinion of the organization or the leader has an impact (as an individual or a group). The public also includes individuals who are interested in the organization and becoming a customer, but are not a customer yet. Their opinions can still have a significant impact. As a follower, we need to listen to the public and put what they are saying into the appropriate context before providing it to the leader and other members of the organization.

Our responsibility is to communicate to all of these groups and summarize the information into something that can be provided to the leader along with recommendations in order to make better decisions.

Ability to Handle Conflict

Implied in the ability to handle conflict, is the patience to allow conflict to develop. Conflict should not be viewed as something to be avoided at all costs. In fact, within organizations or relationships, some level of healthy tension which can lead to conflict is beneficial in order for growth to occur. Muscles of the body need tension in order to stay healthy and grow—so do people. Lou Schuler, fitness author, writes, "Muscles only grow when they're subjected to a certain threshold of tension—that is, they have to be under some kind of strain to grow."[64]

In life, without some sort of tension and conflict there is no challenge or growth and so we atrophy and deteriorate, just like muscles do. Some level of tension, stress, and conflict is required for growth. In the same way, an organization or company without tension or strain to reach a goal that is difficult and challenging will not grow to the next level. Without tension or conflict our gains and successes will be mediocre at best.

As soon as we make the decision to go after a challenging goal or project, there will be tension and often conflict—and as a result, potential for growth and success. We need to anticipate this type of healthy tension and some level of conflict in order to channel the energy and resolution appropriately.

So healthy tension and conflict is good, but as it develops it needs to be resolved or it can become unhealthy. Synergetic Followers understand this and play an important part in allowing healthy tension and conflict develop and then assist in resolving it at the appropriate point and moving on to the next challenge. Going back to our analogy, after stretching a muscle, we need to allow it to relax. This same cycle for building muscle is appropriate for growth in an organization.

Resolving healthy tension and conflict is an important skill for a follower. We can help the organization and our leader by recognizing this tension cycle as an integral part of growth and assisting in the resolution.

Conflict resolution is often left up to the leader to address and not all leaders do it very well. Whatever can be done that does not require escalation to the leader, but continues the growth cycle of the project or organization is a benefit that we can provide. The best teams have developed this culture of welcoming a challenge and working through the tensions and conflicts that arise as a result.

There are thousands of books, videos, and podcasts about resolving conflict, so we won't go into the different methods of conflict resolution in detail here. Resolution usually requires many of the traits that we have already covered (e.g. valuing and respecting others, humility, communication skills) as well as the willingness to confront with respect, identifying the key issues (not the personalities), and working towards a win-win situation.

In summary, communication and handling conflict are not innate skills—they are acquired. These are not abilities that people are born with. There are certainly people who seem to communicate better than others naturally, but often this is because they were raised in an environment where people communicated with each other and provided a model to learn. Regardless of our experience and skill, communication is something that is important for us to learn to do well.

There are thousands of stories of people who overcame language disabilities to become effective communicators. As followers, if we feel weak in this area, that's completely understandable. Let's get to work and learn to communicate and handle conflict better. We can learn through books, videos, watching others, by being guided, coached or mentored. The barriers can sometimes be formidable, but with some hard work and the right help, we can overcome them.

Chapter 21
Ten. Make Decisions Based on Data

Let's take a quick quiz. What president of the United States are we talking about? He was elected to Congress in '46 and then elected to President in '60. He was very concerned with civil rights during his time as president. He was shot in the head and assassinated on a Friday and was succeeded by his Vice President who was from the south. The assassin was killed before he could go to trial for his crime.

Of course we're talking about John F. Kennedy. And we're also talking about Abraham Lincoln—100 years earlier. The information that was needed in order to guess which president was being described is in the paragraph above, but it was incomplete. This is similar to the situations that leaders are faced with all the time. They are provided with inadequate data (often thinking that it is complete) and make their decision based on a partial context and incorrect assumptions they have.

Data-based Decision-Making is the final component of a Synergetic Follower. We can help by providing data in a way that good decisions can be made from the information. These days we have a glut of information online—more than anyone can handle and understand. But just having lots of data doesn't mean that there is understanding of what the information and data indicates or represents. Doing the analysis of the information so that decisions can be made is a key skill that companies and organizations need.

Leaders today are asking for more and more of their decisions to be based on data and information of all types. The old kind of decision-making that was "by the gut" and instinctual is fading into the past. With all of the competition and challenges that are faced today, we can't afford to make the mistakes that could be avoided by looking at the facts and the data. The whole "by the gut" type of decision-making is great for the movies, but it is over-rated in the real world when there is so much information that is readily available to help us make better decisions. The key is to sort out the information in a way that decisions can be made.

Too Much Information

Even with the increased demand for data-based decision making, the leader often has to make the decisions without the appropriate information and data. This is because many followers don't provide information to their leaders in a way that it is prepared for decision-making. Instead they just provide the data. One of the more frustrating situations for a leader is when their staff provide information that still requires the leader to sift through, analyze, create scenarios and options first—and then make a decision. Information is everywhere and there is so much of it, that it is often difficult for leaders to make a decision because they can be literally drowning in data.

This can create a situation that is not that different from the old days when the leader lacked the information necessary to make the decisions. These days there is so much information that some leaders still go with their instinct because there isn't enough time to sort out all of the data (instead of having too little of it). Jay Bourland, head of technology at Pitney Bowes says, "It's a mass of structured, unstructured and real-time data, data in storage, operational data, marketing data, data from external sources, and model, predictive and past-result data. To deal with all of that, you need mechanisms in place to manage it and make sure it's fit for use and that it's being used appropriately."[65]

It's important that the Synergetic Follower assist by working with and analyzing the data so that it is provided to the leader prepared for the decision-making process. This can be accomplished by sifting through the information, looking for trends, patterns, options and scenarios that will assist the leader in making a decision. We can then utilize digital tools, like spreadsheets and charting software, providing the information in a way that the leader can quickly see the key trends and options and then make an informed, intelligent decision.

The information is even more valuable when it is collected from multiple sources and evaluated by others to make sure that the options are as realistic and objective as possible and that the recommendations reflect the analysis.

Decision-based Data

Let's look a little deeper at the type of information that is sometimes provided that is too incomplete to be used to make decisions. For example, let's say we work in a book store and we go tell the owner that we sold 500 books, but the previous month we only sold 400 books. Everyone is really happy about this increase—especially the owner. But what does this information tell us? It tells us very little besides the fact that we sold more books this month than the last month. What caused this increase? Did we put the books on sale (and thereby reduce our profit)? Did we display the best sellers up near the check-out register? Did we advertise differently? Did we have an author come and talk about her new book and as a result sold 100 her books? The answers to each one of these questions would help the owner make a better decision based on better context around the information.

It would seem obvious that people would automatically bring this type of information to the leader, but unfortunately they don't. In fact they usually bring too much information or too little. They bring all the data: how many were sold, what the average price is, how many of each title were sold, what the profit for each book was and for each category of book, how many were sold in the morning and how many in the afternoon, and how many were sold each day and on and on. Some of this information could actually be helpful to the leader. However, when it's dumped on the leader's desk (or sent by email) without any analysis, it is overwhelming to the leader and requires the leader to analyze it (which they don't have time to do).

As a result, the leader won't be able to decide if increasing advertising was the cause of the increase in sales or was it the book author that came in, or perhaps it was the new incentive program instituted for the sales staff or maybe it was the special sale that was done two weekends in a row. Did those increased sales come from a particular zip code? Perhaps a direct mail advertisement to people living in that zip code could be very effective. We'll never know, because the leader looks at all the data and isn't sure where to start and doesn't really have the time to do the analysis. As a result, many leaders put the mountain of data to the side for another day and are happy that sales are up regardless of the reason.

We've talked about providing too little or too much information that creates an environment where decision-making is difficult. Let's now look at the kinds of filtering of information that would be helpful to decision-making. Take for instance the bookstore that sold 500 books one month and sold only 400 books the previous month. The following questions could be asked and the answers synthesized and provided to the leader to help make a decision:

- What are the trends over a six-month period?
- What did we sell last year at this time?
- What are the characteristics of the customers that made a purchase?
- What type of promotion did we have the previous month vs. any promotion this month?
- Were there any events nearby this month that might have increased foot traffic in the store?
- Looking at the books we sold, was there an increase in one title or author or category of book?

After these and other questions have been researched and analyzed, there are a number of conclusions can be drawn from them and trends that would cause us to change things for improved sales in the future.

Presenting information for decision-making is critical. In Terry Jay Fadem's book on the art of asking questions, he outlines eight basic elements that are crucial to asking a better question about information that will lead to results, starting with these three, "1. What do we know? 2. What do we not know? and 3. What are our objectives?"[66] We have to ask the right kinds of questions and get the answers before presenting information to the leader.

Charts vs. Spreadsheets

We can't just give the leader a spreadsheet with numbers on it. It is very difficult to pull out trends from a spreadsheet.

However, if we create a chart from the numbers, the trends and indicators often become obvious.

Numbers are important because they show exact quantities. But it is the charts and pictures that show trends and relationships between the numbers. Charts will show relationships that are invisible to us if we just look at a spreadsheet of numbers. Some leaders like the details, but most prefer higher-level charts and trends so they can see direction and the relationships in the data. These relationships and trends help the leader make the "big" decisions, which are critical to the organization's success.

Providing multiple options

Once we've provided information and data that is better-suited for making decisions, we want to follow that up with a few scenarios/options and a recommendation.

Providing multiple options and scenarios gives the leader choices—which also assists in framing the issue. For example, we might tell the leader that, "We have a couple of options, we could invest in advertising across the city. Or we could invest in five key zip codes, which is a little riskier, but might have more promise based on the demographics and the past sales history." Identifying conservative and riskier scenarios gives them a range of options. In addition, providing some advantages and disadvantages to each option helps the leader see some of the promise and the downsides of the decisions that they may not have thought of.

After providing the different scenarios or options we should provide a recommendation. For example, we might recommend, "Looking at the options, we think that advertising in these five key zip codes is more promising than our other options." This tells the leader that we've done some analysis and have thought more deeply about the issue than just providing the data and some options.

Providing analysis, implications, recommendations and a few potential scenarios/options is the kind of work that most leaders are always wishing for. The good leader will look at the analysis and research, the options that are available and the recommendation—and begin to develop a trust in our work.

No-Win Scenario

Sometimes the options/scenarios are all undesirable and there isn't a "good" option to recommend. Many people go to the leader in this situation and say, "there's nothing we can do." This doesn't really help the leader. If there are only bad choices to make, then we need to analyze and research those options. By identifying the negative implications for each one and then make a recommendation of the best of the worst choices. The leader recognizes that many times when a decision reaches the top, that it is a difficult one, often without a positive outcome. Even categorizing the options into: #1=Bad, #2=Worse, #3=Horrible, #4=Unforgiveable, makes the leader's decision easier. Leaders need options and choices (we all do). The Synergetic Follower researches, analyzes, identifies options and provides a recommendation.

So far we have been talking mostly about decisions the leader needs to make. There are, as we mentioned earlier, a lot of decisions that are appropriate for us and the staff below us.

Decisions made by followers can have a major impact on the outcome of a project. As Peter Drucker reminds us, "Most discussions of decision making assume that only senior executives make decisions or that only senior executives' decisions matter. This is a dangerous mistake."

There are many situations where we are the right person to make the decision and it doesn't need to go to the leader. Now if we have a "micro-manager" that wants to be involved in every little decision that is made, then that's a different issue (perhaps it's time to find a leader that trusts us a little more).

When we have a situation where the choices have been identified and analyzed and we've worked with the leader enough to know what they would do in this particular situation, it's important to make the decision instead of pushing it up to the leader to decide. If a decision is obvious, why waste the leader's time? In many situations the leader doesn't even need to or want to be informed (this doesn't mean hiding decision that they should know about). Make sure that the documentation of the process and the decision is recorded somewhere.

Leaders should be making the toughest, most difficult decisions—the ones that have the greatest impact. Since the life of a leader is filled with making uncertain decisions, any assistance we can provide through research, analysis, identifying implications and providing recommendations will be valued.

Chapter 22
What we can learn from Leaders

There are many benefits that come from following a good leader. These include dealing with others, how to handle conflict, what to do with people that don't like you, setting goals and teamwork.

Working with others

Leaders, at least the good ones, know how to work with others. It's usually what got them into the leadership position in the first place (it's the price they pay). The top leaders are all about relationships and numbers. They develop a strong team that works together well and holds the team accountable for the numbers (whether they are sales forecasts, on-time deliveries, or units produced). It will be helpful to observe how the leader interacts with their colleagues/peers and set things up so that the team can be successful.

This includes the types of relationships the leader builds and even the way the leader deals with annoying people or difficult people. Successful leadership (and followership) involves working well with a diverse group of individuals to form a well-functioning team.

How to deal with conflict

Leaders often deal with conflict as part of their everyday life. As we watch the leader in different situations we will learn how they deal with minor conflicts. Occasionally we will see how the leader handles significant crises that cause stress. There will even be opportunities over time to observe the leader in an emergency situation.

How to deal with people that don't like you

We all like to have people like us and it sometimes surprises us (and our mother) when they don't. However, good leaders have to deal with people who don't like them on a regular basis. This includes internal staff, customers or constituents and even the public, including the media. John Maxwell, author of many leadership books says, "As a leader, if I try to please everybody, eventually I will alienate everybody. A leader must be true to the vision and the people—even when it's not popular."[67] Being able to watch a good leader deal with people who are not supportive of who they are or what they do is important to the Synergetic Follower. Much can be learned from observing how the leader handles these situations.

How to set goals

Learning from the leader on how they set goals and accomplish them is critical for future success. We can learn a lot by watching the leader establish the goals, identify the project or processes that will lead to completion, find the resources and staff necessary to achieve the goal, assign the different tasks and put it all together in way that accomplishes the goal.

How to build a team

Good leaders build good teams, but it's not easy. Watching the leader select members of the team (and learning why they picked each individual), how they delegate assignments, how the vision is created for the team and the structure of how the team will be working together is very important for us to know. Observing how the leader establishes communication with the team through status reports, email, phone calls, task assignments and how the team communicates with each other will also be helpful. William Dyer and JeffereyDyer describe the evolution of a team's leadership in their book, *Team building: proven strategies for improving team perfor-*

mance, "As the team matures and as the leader shifts more responsibility for team functioning from his or her shoulders to the team, the team leader's role begins to change from educator to one of being a coach."[68] The Synergetic Follower recognizes this process and helps the leader move from educator to coach of a new team.

How to deal with success or failure

At the end of a project, watching how the leader handles success or failure will tell us a lot about them. If the leader takes all the credit for the successes and blames others on the failures, we may want to start looking for a new leader. It's unfortunate that there are still leaders that behave this way, but we see it all the time.

Failure, as we'll discuss further, is a key component of growth, learning, and ultimately success. **Without failure, no organization/company can be successful. How we deal with failure will decide what our future will look like.**

On the other hand, if the leader shares success with the team and takes responsibility (at least in public) for failures, then we have someone worthy of following and investing our efforts in. The best leaders will show others how to handle success and failures, while learning from both.

Chapter 23
Represent and Recruit

When we choose to follow a leader, we automatically become a representative of the team, organization and leader (whether we want to or not). Too often we assume that everyone is watching just the leader, but a lot of people watch to see who the leader gathers around them. **We can tell a lot about the leader by looking at the followers. Great leaders have great followers.** If the followers work as a team, accomplish their goals and have the traits of a Synergetic Follower, then we know that the leader is talented. The followers represent the leader.

There are times when we are asked specifically to represent the leader. For example, we may be asked to go and speak to a group or attend an event on behalf of leader. We need to make sure we're prepared, in fact, over-prepared. This includes being prepared to respond to questions about the mission and organization that we are representing. We want to be thoughtful and respectful because people are looking at us as a representative of the leader. However, our goal is not to attract attention to ourselves, but to help them understand the mission of the organization and our leader. As we mentioned, this is not just when we think people are watching, but all the time. In the digital age of video cameras and cell phone cameras, someone is always watching.

As we mentioned, Synergetic Followers try to avoid the spotlight and do most of their work behind the scenes. However, if we do get into a situation where the light falls on us for something we did and people see our work and start asking us about it, then there are a few things that we can do.

For example, in the movie *Bull Durham*, Kevin Costner's character Crash Davis, mentors a younger baseball player who is headed to the big leagues with some key clichés to use when being interviewed:

1. We gotta play 'em one day at a time.
2. I'm just happy to be here. Hope I can help the ballclub.
3. I just want to give it my best shot, and the good Lord willing, things will work out.

Now these suggestions from *Bull Durham* are a bit tongue-in-cheek, but it's true that sports stars know the rules about being a member of a team. If you look around a little bit, you'll see quotes from every successful sports hero talking about the team:

> "Talent wins games, but teamwork and intelligence wins championships." – Michael Jordan, NBA Basketball Player

> "Finding good players is easy. Getting them to play as a team is another story." – Casey Stengel, AL Baseball Coach

> "I am a member of a team, and I rely on the team, I defer to it and sacrifice for it, because the team, not the individual, is the ultimate champion." – Mia Hamm, World Cup Soccer Player

> "People who work together will win, whether it be against complex football defenses or the problems of modern society." – NFL Coach Vince Lombardi

The following three suggestions help keep the focus on the leader and on the team.

1. Point to our leader who supported the effort. The reality is that without the leader's support we wouldn't be able to accomplish the things that we're doing.

2. Point to the team, to the other members we have been working with. We see sports heroes do this all the time on interviews. They don't talk much about their own efforts, but talk about the team effort instead.

3. Don't talk too long. Don't go on and on about the team or ourselves. The world is filled with people who talk forever and don't say anything. We need to choose our words wisely and say them and then move on.

Although they often represent leaders, many followers are also leaders in other areas of their lives. That leadership area could be in something as specific and defined as their family or being on a community board or task force. Synergetic Followers accomplish great things without being in charge. They go to bed at night and are very satisfied with everything that was accomplished that day and they leave behind a rich legacy of significant achievements.

Recruit

One of the tasks that we have is to recruit others into the team or organization. If we believe in the leader and mission, then it will be natural to promote both and tell others about why we're involved. Our focus is to share the mission and talk about the leader. Recruiting is an important skill for the Synergetic Follower. Before we recruit, identify the good things about our organization and/or leader. We need to make sure we communicate that information in a compelling and respectful way. Think about open positions or volunteer opportunities that someone you know might fit and then begin recruiting.

Leaders are always looking for good followers—and so are Synergetic Followers. Instead of waiting for the leader to identify someone to fill a spot, we can assist the leader in identifying the perfect candidate. We shouldn't hesitate putting a potential individual forward to be considered if we truly believe in them. Leaders like to have choices, especially if there are potential candidates that we have recruited and have gone through our screening. People are the most valuable resource an organization/business has. If we find people we know or have recruited that can be a valuable contributor, it will really help both the leader and the organization.

Once a candidate has been recruited by us and hired it is also our responsibility to mentor them if the organization allows it. We should help them, guide them, and assist them in getting acquainted with the organization and the staff. Additionally, we should also help them understand and develop into a Synergetic Follower. Since we recruited them, we want to help make them successful in the same way that we are helping the leader be successful.

Supporting

Let's remember that good leaders are focused on the mission, the organization, and major projects. They are looking for others to join up with them and work with them to achieve the goals.

Occasionally there are leaders that are more interested in having followers focused on the leader—and not on the mission or goals of the company/organization. If we find ourselves with a leader like that, we may want to look around for alternatives. Leaders that are focused on having groupies, usually don't have a big impact or a long lifespan with the company.

Chapter 24
A Few More Benefits to Being a
Synergetic Follower

While the objective is to help the leader and the organiza-tion/company achieve their goals, there are also a few more benefits that we didn't mention earlier that come from being a follower. As we look at a few of these less important ben-efits, several of them will seem shallow—and they probably are. It's one of the reasons we put this chapter near the end of the book.

However, despite the trivial nature of a couple of these, let's at least review some of these additional benefits of being a follower. In these situations we are talking about benefits that come from following a good leader as compared to a weak or untalented one.

Employment Security

While the world is always looking for great leaders, it's also true that strong leaders are always looking for strong followers. If you look at the staff of a successful leader, you will find that many of them have been with the leader for years—often switching companies or organizations with the leader each time they make a move. This is not just due to the comfort of having someone around that you are familiar with, but because true leadership recognizes the benefit of having good followers.

As a result, an individual who is a Synergetic Follower rarely needs to look for employment. In fact, it's quite the opposite. **Talented leaders are always recruiting new followers or trying to retain the followers that they already have.** They understand that their success is tied to their ability to get the right kind of staff on their team.

Less Risk

Leaders are in the limelight and are more visible to others, which usually makes them more of a target for those that are looking to shoot someone down (which sometimes seems like everyone). We all face risk and tough decisions every day, but the leader does them in public and they are judged by the decisions they make.

The key phrase is, "less risk," not "zero risk." There is risk in everything and a follower who is engaged in a project has risk as well. But let's face the facts, the leader is more at risk and the consequences of failure are more public.

Assuming we like our leader and want to stay where we are, we can also lower our risk level by helping the leader be successful, while staying out of the spotlight. When we try to share the stage with the leader, we actually put ourselves at more risk (another reason to keep a low profile). Let the leader get the public applause. We can help shape and implement the project behind the scenes in a way that ensures it succeeds. We don't need to take credit for it.

Share in the Leader's Success

Another benefit of being a good follower is that we are able to share in the fruits of success. Granted, the leader may get paid more (a lot more), have more photos taken, give more speeches, and travel to exotic locations—but who needs all of that? Especially when it comes with so much risk, stress, and shortens our lifespan?

How many millionaire followers whose names we've never heard of were created at companies like Microsoft, Google,

Cisco? These are just some of the more recognizable corporations and there are thousands of companies and organizations around the country that have experienced outstanding success that don't make the national headlines like those businesses have. Behind the leaders of these successful companies are an outstanding team of followers who have benefited from their efforts and the vision of the leader.

While the world seems to fawn over celebrities of all types, let's remember that fame and fortune aren't all they are made out to be. In fact those two rather narrow measures of success rate lower than most of the items on the list of things that make life worth living. We can have an abundant life, make a significant contribution to the world, and still have the time to love our family and develop authentic relationships. If you look at the lives of the rich and famous, most of them don't seem that happy. Headlines shout out stories of celebrities of all vocations that are alcohol- or drug-dependent, have broken families, and have hundreds or thousands of people who don't like them. Anonymity has its benefits.

Synergetic Followers have figured out how to find a good organization and leader to follow and they quietly (well, at least most of the time) contribute to the success of the organization and also shares in that success.

Be with the Leader

There are some people who may not see "being with the leader" as a benefit. If that is the case, then it could mean they have chosen the wrong leader. We may be "working" for a leader, but if we don't buy-in to their leadership, then we're likely not going to get the benefit from being around the leader.

There are many benefits for a follower in being with the leader. Let's look at three of those:

1. Learning from the leader at close range
2. Traveling with the leader
3. Meeting others while with the leader

Learning from the leader at close range

Many good followers become leaders or are already leaders in another area. Learning about leadership from a talented leader at close range is a rare opportunity. This up-close situation allows us to see both good and bad decisions as well as how the leader handles them. Often all that we see is the public view of the leader or even a less-public view when they are in large company meetings or brief hallway encounters.

That's a completely different view compared to the one we see in the leader's office when a large sales contract falls through or there is a crisis in the company. The pressure of being a leader is often minimized, but when it's viewed from a short distance the pressure can not only be seen, but felt.

In addition, seeing how the leader handles good times as well as bad is important. Do they share the credit of the success, spend too much time celebrating the win, or become self-absorbed? This close-up view provides a unique learning lab environment that many followers will point to as key to their success.

Traveling with the leader

Due to the more public aspects of a leader's job, travel is often a common occurrence. Traveling with the leader produces another unique view of how they operate in a less formal or familiar environment. How does the leader handle the stress of traveling, including flight delays, unavailability of rental cars or hotel rooms, and bad service? If the travel is to a customer's site, how does the leader react to complaints, problems and meeting new faces at the customer site? How does the leader respond in a meeting when they are not in charge?

Of course there are other positive aspects to traveling with the leader. Talented leaders are in high demand by customers in addition to others who want to learn from them, which can take them to interesting locations. Besides just learning more about the leader, we also have the opportunity to see places we might not normally visit. Even if the travel is some-times to locations that we weren't interested in visiting, there are always unexpected benefits where we least expect to find them.

Meeting others while with the leader

As a leader, the circle of friends and acquaintances is usu-ally different than the follower's is and creates an opportunity for us to expand our network. This connection with other leaders and individuals can be very helpful in providing ad-ditional opportunities.

Let's not forget that meeting others while traveling with the leader, locally or beyond, can be fascinating and instruc-tional. Sure, there are always those irritating individuals that invade the circle, but most of the time there are interesting individuals who we would never meet except through the leader.

Chapter 25
Failure is Part of Success

Failure is part of the process

After the movie *Apollo 13* came out, it seemed everyone was saying a favorite line from the movie, "Failure is not an option." However in reality, failure is not only an option, it's a requirement. In the movie, the mission had already failed multiple times by the time that statement was made. But there were no other options for failure left at that point, if the crew was to be saved. The good news is that the past successes and failures of the engineers working on the problem in the Apollo mission paid off and they were able to provide a solution that saved the crew.

One of the standard interview questions for a new employee is, "Tell us about the time you failed." I have been in several interview situations where we asked the job candidate to describe a recent failure. If a candidate couldn't remember a failure, they didn't have much of a chance at getting the job. After all, if they didn't really have any recent failures, then they obviously lacked the experience we were looking for. But if they did have failures but couldn't remember them, then it's likely they weren't being honest (we usually remember our failures even more than our successes).

Failure is integral to the success of any major effort. If we're honest, most of our learning comes during the "failure" part of our work, not from the success part. It's during the times of failure that we "learn" and we learn how to adjust, so that the next time we won't fail (or maybe the time after that). Tom Peters, the effervescent and sometimes outrageous author of many business books recommends, "It's a good idea: 'test fast, fail fast, adjust fast' must become the organization's battlecry."[69] This cycle of trying something, failing, then adjusting and trying again is how most of us learn. If we take out the "fail fast" part, then there isn't any learning, we just got lucky with our first try.

While we can learn from any failure, some are more painful than others. Obviously there is a difference between an "epic failure" and a "minor flaw." When an epic failure occurs, sometimes the adjustment is a reorganization of the department/company. Minor flaws are just seen as part of the improvement process and rarely described as a failure. It's all of those failures in-between that cause learning to be so difficult and sometimes painful.

Think of a few famous failed products where the businesses survived despite the failure. For example, the Sony Betamax, Polaroid Instant Movies, the Apple Lisa computer, New Coke, the IBM PC Jr., and the Ford Edsel.

Then there are the examples of famous people who overcame failure in their life to be successful:

1. Henry Ford, whose first two automobile companies failed

2. John Wayne, who was rejected from the United States Naval Academy

3. Bill Gates, who dropped out of Harvard

4. Albert Einstein, whose grades were so poor that one of his teachers suggested he quit school

5. Michael Jordan, who was cut from his high school basketball team for lack of skill

6. John Grisham, whose first book was rejected by sixteen agents and twelve publishing houses

7. Walt Disney, who was fired by a newspaper editor for his lack of ideas

Failure is an American tradition—our country was built on entrepreneurship, taking risks and learning from failure.

When you let the leader down

Many of the small failures aren't even noticed by the leader (or others for that matter). But some failures are not only noticed by the leader, but impact the leader's goals as well. This is bound to happen occasionally, unless we don't take any risks (but if we don't take risks that can cause other issues).

When we let the leader down, we need to make sure we do three things:

1. Make sure we discuss the situation with the leader. Just because we know that the leader knows, doesn't mean that's enough. It's important to bring the issue to closure.

2. Identify the learning that comes from the failure. Review what happened and identify what could have been done differently or better.

3. Put processes in place for the future, so that the chances of a similar failure is reduced or eliminated.

Leaders fail as well—except their failures are usually more public. With the right kind of leader, the Synergetic Follower will develop a true collaborative relationship partnership that celebrates success and learns from failure.

189

15 minutes of self-pity

I remember a failure to meet an important deadline a number of years ago. As I wrestled with the impact, the president of the company called me and discussed the situation. She then said she understood how disappointing it was. In fact, she suggested that I engage in a healthy 15 minutes of self-pity and grieving. Then get over it and move on. It was (and still is) good advice.

Failure is bound to happen. How we deal with it is important. Brush it off too casually and it tells others (and ourselves) that we really weren't very invested in seeing it succeed. But sometimes we can swing too far the other direction and become depressed and reluctant to try anything challenging again (fear of failure). That's not healthy either. Take the 15 minutes. Have a good cry if that helps. Then dust yourself off and get going again. You'll be smarter and more prepared for the obstacles that come your way the next time—and more likely to succeed.

How do you respond to failure?

Failure doesn't determine who you are—how you respond to failure does. **Failure is part of life, more so for most of us than success is. How we respond to it is critical to our ability to adjust, move forward, and succeed on the next try.**

J.K. Rowling, best-selling author of the Harry Potter books, said at her Harvard Commencement Address in June of 2008, "You might never fail on the scale I did, but some failure in life is inevitable. It is impossible to live without failing at something, unless you live so cautiously that you might as well not have lived at all—in which case, you fail by default."[70] Her response to failure produced success after success.

After we fail, we should spend a few minutes in reflection. Then recognize that the world is somehow moving forward anyway despite our failure. We need to get over it, review what we have learned, make the appropriate adjustments, and tackle the next goal.

Chapter 26
Famous Leaders that had a Great Follower

Leaders and Followers

Leadership is discussed in a thousand books, movies, television and radio shows, blogs and tweets. Let's take a quick look at a few of the famous leaders who had a great follower (or second-in-command). Their names are in bold print and articles are written about them: Walt Disney, Bill Gates, Steve Jobs, Samuel Johnson, and Joe Montana. However, where would these great leaders be without key followers. Where would Walt Disney be without the financial genius of his brother Roy or Bill Gates without Steve Ballmer to sell the software or Steve Jobs without Steve Wozniak who designed and built the Apple II or Samuel Johnson without James Boswell to write about him or Joe Montana without Dwight Clark to catch all those passes?

By definition, a leader requires that there be followers. As the old leadership proverb says, if you call yourself a leader and no one is following, you are just out for a walk. When we talk about a "follower," we're talking about someone who has made a choice to follow someone and is engaged in the mission/vision that the leader is part of. Let's take a look at a few of the more popular real-life examples of followers who are second-in-command to the top leader.

Steve Jobs has, over time, proven that he has what it takes to be a leader. However, without his friend Steve Wozniak (aka the Woz), who was an engineer and designed and built the Apple I and II, we might never have heard of the other Steve. Steve Wozniak was working as a young engineer at HP when he met Steve Jobs who had a summer job at HP. Jobs sold his VW Van and convinced Woz to sell his HP Calculator to provide startup funds for their new company, Apple Computer—the rest is history.

What if Wozniak had refused to follow Steve Jobs? Would he have found someone else to follow him and build the Apple I or II? Maybe . . . maybe not. The main point here is that Steve Wozniak chose to follow the leadership of Steve Jobs and it made all the difference for both of them.

In the music industry, few bands have been as successful as U2 and its high-profile lead vocalist, Bono. Yet the lead guitarist, David Evans, also known as The Edge, is one of the principal songwriters for the band. He is one of the most influential guitar players of our time and writes music for other projects including major motion pictures. Unlike Bono, who is viewed by most as the leader of the band, The Edge is largely unknown outside of the music world. What would U2 be like without his contribution? The Edge ranks #24 on Rolling Stone's Greatest Guitarists of all time and he provides a distinctive sound to U2 in addition to the songwriting. Bono might have made it as a solo act, but it's doubtful he would have achieved the fame and success that he has had without The Edge.

This concept of the importance of followers is not a new phenomenon, but is ancient as time itself. Most people have heard of Socrates and his teachings (e.g. the Socratic Method), but Socrates, who lived around 400 BC, never wrote anything (at least not anything that we've ever found). Instead we know all about Socrates through his followers who wrote about him, foremost among them is Plato. Socrates was his mentor and Plato wrote more about his mentor than anyone else and is considered to have provided the most comprehensive and reliable information on Socrates.

Although there were some other contemporaries of Plato that wrote about Socrates, including Aristotle and Xenophon, their works were much smaller than Plato's. If Plato had not followed Socrates, there is a good chance that we wouldn't know much about him and the Socratic Method might have been called something else. This is a good example of how a follower provides influence and in this case, a permanent place in history to the leader.

Let's look at one more example, Michael Eisner and Frank Wells. People recognize Michael Eisner as the former long-term Chairman and CEO of the Walt Disney Company. Most people don't know who Frank Wells was (he was killed in a 1994 helicopter crash). Even fewer people know that he was appointed President of Disney on the same day that Eisner became CEO. They were both recruited by several large investors (including Roy Disney Jr. and Stanley Gold) who were trying to turn Disney around in the early 1980's. Some felt that Wells, as President of Warner Brothers, should be the top man and CEO. As Eisner recalls in that first meeting with Wells and the top investors, "I will never forget when Roy Disney and Stanley Gold put us together to discuss coming to Disney. Being a little cocky, I suggested I become CEO. Without hesitation Frank said OK. I was stunned. 'Did you say yes?' I asked. He said, 'yup' and that was that. From that moment on I knew he was special."[71]

Wells only took moments to accept the second-in-command follower position. For 30 years he carried a crinkled slip of paper from a fortune cookie that said, "Humility is the final achievement." He understood one of the rules of being a great follower—you have to be humble.

During Wells' 10 years with Disney, revenues went from $1.5 billion to $8.5 billion and the stock value increased 1,500%. While Eisner was in front of the cameras and providing the creative vision that Disney needed, Wells was behind the scene negotiating megadeals and managing the finances, the operations, the studios and everything else to ensure its success. How important was Wells contribution? Priceless according to many. Looking at just one financial measurement, Disney went from a high 11.4% net profit margin in 1995 (the year after Wells death), down to 0.5% only 10 years later when Eisner resigned in 2005 under pressure from the same Board members and investors that had hired both of them.

Chapter 27
Making the Decision

This will be our shortest chapter, because the message is simple, we just need to make the decision. Let's stop "working" for someone else and make the decision to be a Synergetic Follower—someone who changes the world. Take a look around you—is this where you want to be? Is this the leader you want to follow? Is this the company or organization or movement you want to contribute to and invest your life in?

Our choice of who to follow is critical to the success of the leader and the organization, but we don't always believe it. We think to ourselves, "what can one person like me do? What impact can I possibly have?"

Jim Collins, the author of "Good to Great" reminds us, "Greatness is not a function of circumstance. Greatness, it turns out, is largely a matter of conscious choice, and discipline."[72] Make the choice.

We need to look around and find the organization and leader that fits us—and then start following in a new way. It will transform our world.

Notes

Introduction

[1] "synergetic," Collins English Dictionary - Complete & Unabridged 10th Edition (HarperCollins Publishers), accessed May 7, 2011, http://dictionary.reference.com/browse/synergetic.

[2] Ira Chaleff, The courageous follower: standing up to & for our leaders (San Francisco: Berrett-Koehler Publishers, 2009).

[3] Ronald E. Riggio, Ira Chaleff, and Jean Lipman-Blumen. The art of followership: how great followers create great leaders and organizations, (Hoboken: Jossey-Bass Inc Pub, 2008).

Chapter 1

[4] Center for Disease Control (CDC), "Malaria," accessed June 26, 2011, http://www.cdc.gov/malaria/about/history.

[5] Discoveries in Medicine, "Interferon" (accessed June 26, 2011). http://www.discoveriesinmedicine.com/Hu-Mor/Interferon.html

[6] Niccolò Machiavelli, The Prince, trans. Harvey Mansfield (Chicago: University of Chicago Press, 1985).

Chapter 2

[7] Mayrav, "LAT's Scathing Internal Memo. Read It Here," accessed January 26, 2007, http://www.mediabistro.com/fishbowl-LA/on/lats_scathing_internal_memo_read_it_here_51895.asp.

[8] Tom Koppel, Powering the Future: The Ballard Fuel Cell and the Race to Change the World (Hoboken: John Wiley & Sons Inc, 2001), 85.

[9] Paul Israel, Edison: A Life of Invention (Hoboken: John Wiley & Sons, 2000).

[10] Margaret Mead and Robert Textor, The World Ahead: An Anthropologist Anticipates the Future (New York: Berghahn Books, 2005), 12.

Chapter 3

[11] Peters,Tom. The Pursuit of Wow! Every Person's Guide to Topsy-Turvy Times. New York: Vintage, 1994.

[12] Dickens,Charles. The Complete Christmas Books of Charles Dickens. Lawrence, KS: Digireads.com, 2009.

[13] Star Wars: Episode IV - A New Hope, Film, Directed by George Lucas, 1977.

[14] Boris Groysberg, Ashish Nanda, and Nitin Nohria. "The Risky Business of Hiring Stars." Harvard Business Review, May 2004.

[15] Ibid.

Chapter 4

[16] Radicati Group, "Email Statistics Report 2009-2013," last modified May 6, 2009, accessed Jul 1, 2010, ,http://www.radicati.com/wp/wp-content/uploads/2009/05/e-mail-statistics-report-2009-pr.pdf.

[17] Ingram, "Matthew," last modified Jan 14, 2011, accessed Jul 1, 2011, http://gigaom.com/2011/01/14/was-what-happened-in-tunisia-a-twitter-revolution.

Chapter 5

[18] Wikipedia, "Linus Torvalds," accessed July June 30, 2011, http://en.wikipedia.org/wiki/Linus_Torvalds

[19] The H, "Linus Torvalds named one of the 100 most influential inventors," last modified Feb 2010, accessed Feb 15, 2010 http://www.h-online.com/open/news/item/Linus-Torvalds-named-one-of-the-100-most-influential-inventors-922622.html.

[20] Boardmember.com, The Volatility Report, accessed, June 20, 2010 http://www.boardmember.com/WorkArea/linkit.aspx?LinkIdentifier=id&ItemID=3366

Chapter 6

[21] William Pretzer, Working at Inventing: Thomas A. Edison and the Menlo Park Experience (Baltimore: Johns Hopkins Univ Pr, 2002), 4.

[22] John Wooden, The Essential Wooden: A Lifetime of Lessons on Leaders and Leadership (New York: McGraw-Hill, 2006), 120.

[23] Muoio, Anna. "My Greatest Lesson." Fast Company, May 1998.

[24] Lauren Dugan, "Useful twitter account of the week@neiltyson," All Twitter, last modified April 5, 2011, accessed May 8, 2011, http://www.mediabistro.com/alltwitter/useful-twitter-account-of-the-week-neiltyson_b8112.

[25] www.salary.com, "Employee Job Satisfaction & Retention Survey," Salary.com, last modified 2008, accessed May 2011, www.salary.com/docs/resources/JobSatSurvey_08.pdf.

[26] Joey Green, The Road to Success is Paved with Failure (New York: Little, Brown and Company, 2001), 1.

Chapter 7

[27] John Wooden, They Call Me Coach (New York: McGraw-Hill, 2003), 62.

[28] David Giles, Illusions of immortality: a psychology of fame and celebrity (Basingstoke, England: Palgrave Macmillan, 2000), 143.

Chapter 8

[29] Barbara Kellerman, Bad leadership: what it is, how it happens, why it matters, Harvard Business Press, 2004, 39.

[30] Adams, Scott, The Dilbert principle: a cubicle's-eye view of bosses, meetings, management fads & other workplace afflictions, (New York: Harper Paperbacks, 1997), 14.

Chapter 9

[31] Walker Information, "1999 National Business Ethics Study," Walker Information in association with the Hudson Institute, last modified Sep 1999, http://www.bentley.edu/cbe/research/surveys/19.cfm.

[32] Hill, Napoleon, Think and Grow Rich (Bnpublishing.Com, 2007), 70.

[33] Rich Karlgaard, "World's Worst Disease," Digital Rules, accessed May 22, 2011, (Forbes.com, Sep 1, 2006), http://www.forbes.com/global/2006/0109/035A.html.

Chapter 10

[34] Alex Pattakos, Prisoners of Our Thoughts: Viktor Frankl's Principles for Discovering Meaning in Life and Work: Easyread Large Edition, (Read How You Want.Com, 2008), 88.

[35] John Baldoni, Great communication secrets of great leaders (McGraw-Hill Professional, 2003), 83.

[36] Nancy Collins, "Gotcha!," New York Magazine, May 25, 1987, 28.

[37] Seth Godin, May 26, 2011, "Looking for the right excuse," Seth's Blog, http://sethgodin.typepad.com/seths_blog/2011/05/excuse-112.html.

Chapter 11

[38] Norman Vincent Peale, The Power of Positive Thinking: 10 Traits for Maximum Results (New York: Simon & Schuster, 2003).

Chapter 12

[39] Peter Drucker, The Five Most Important Questions You Will Ever Ask About Your Organization (Jossey-Bass, 2008), 2.

40 The Conference Board, "U.S. Job Satisfaction at Lowest Level in Two Decades," The Conference Board, January 5, 2010.

41 Abraham Maslow, Motivation and Personality (New York: Harper, 1954).

42 James Collins, Good to great: why some companies make the leap—and others don't (New York: Harperbusiness, 2001).

Chapter 13

43 Edward Lawler and James O'Toole, America at Work: Choices and Challenges (Basingstoke, UK: Palgrave MacMillan, 2008), 5

44 Rupert Lee, The eureka! moment: 100 key scientific discoveries of the 20th century (Brandon, VT: Psychology Press, 2002), 237.

Chapter 14

45 Marcus Buckingham and Donald Clifton, Now, discover your strengths (New York: Simon & Schuster, 2001).

46 John McKnight, John Kretzmann, Northwestern University, and Neighborhood Innovations, Building communities from the inside out: a path toward finding and mobilizing a community's assets (Acta Publishing, 1993).

47 Dirty Jobs, Television, June 4, 2011 (Discovery Channel).

Chapter 15

[48] Seth Godin, Linchpin: Are You Indispensable? (London: Penguin, 2010).

[49] David Allen, Getting Things Done: The Art of Stress-Free Productivity (London: Penguin Group USA, 2001).

Chapter 16

[50] Debra Meyerson, and Joyce Fletcher, "A Modest Manifesto for Shattering the Glass Ceiling," Harvard Business Review, Jan/Feb 2000, 135.

[51] Mark Leary, The curse of the self: self-awareness, egotism, and the quality of human life (Oxford: Oxford University Press, USA, 2004), 167.

[52] James Collins, Good to great: why some companies make the leap—and others don't (New York: Harperbusiness, 2001), 21.

Chapter 17

[53] Stephen M. R.Covey, Speed Of Trust (New York: Free Press, 2008), 1.

[54] Kevin Freiberg and Jackie Freiberg, Nuts!: Southwest Airlines' crazy recipe for business and personal success (New York: Crown Publishing, 1998), 304.

[55] Ira Chaleff, The courageous follower: standing up to & for our leaders (San Francisco: Berrett-Koehler Publishers, 2009).

Chapter 18

[56] Anita Pankake, Implementation: making things happen (Larchmont, NY: Eye On Education, Inc., 1998), 75.

[57] Michael Crews and Ed Sweet, Hard Work: Success Made Easy (Escondido, CA: SDG Press Books, 2004), 204

Chapter 19

[58] Eric Bloom, Manager Mechanics: Tips and Advice for First-Time Managers (Bloomington, IN: iUniverse, 2009), 47.

[59] Brett Simmons, Sep 9, 2009, "Courage to Participate in Transformation of the Leader." Brett L. Simmons Blog, www.bretl-simmons.com/2009-09/courage-to-participate-in-transformation-of-the-leader.

[60] Nicholas Machiavelli, The Historical, Political, and Diplomatic Writings of Niccolo Machiavelli (Charleston: Nabu Press, 2010).

[61] Suzanne Bates, Motivate Like a CEO: Communicate Your Strategic Vision and Inspire *People to Act!* (Hightstown, NJ: McGraw-Hill Professional, 2008), 114

[62] Hans Finzel, The Top Ten Mistakes Leaders Make (Colorado Springs: David C Cook, 2007), 109.

Chapter 20

[63] Michael Purdy and Deborah Borisoff, Listening in everyday life: a personal and professional approach (Lanham, Maryland: University Press of America, 1997), 248.

[64] Lou Schuler and Alwyn Cosgrove, The new rules of lifting: six basic moves for maximum muscle (New York: Avery Publishing Group, 2006), 59.

Chapter 21

[65] Ed Sperling, "Too Much Data," Forbes.com Nov 16, 2009, accessed Jun 20, 2011, http://www.forbes.com.

[66] Terry Jay Fadem, The art of asking: ask better questions, get better answers (Upper Saddle River, NJ: FT Press, 2008), 4.

Chapter 22

[67] John Maxwell, Leadership gold: lessons learned from a lifetime of leading (Nashville, TN: Thomas Nelson Inc, 2008), 136.

[68] William Dyer and Jeffrey Dyer, Team building: proven strategies for improving team performance (San Francisco, CA: Jossey-Bass Inc Pub, 2007), 63.

Chapter 25

[69] Thomas Peters, Thriving on chaos: handbook for a management revolution (New York : Harper Paperbacks, 1987), 480.

[70] J. K. Rowling, June 5, 2008, "Harvard Commencement Address" (Harvard University, Boston, MA).

Chapter 26

[71] Jeff Kober, April 2, 2009, "Celebrating Frank Wells," Mouse-Planet, accessed Jun 28,2011, http://www.mouseplanet. com/8780/Celebrating_Frank_Wells

Chapter 27

[72] James Collins, Good to great and the social sectors: why business thinking is not the answer : a monograph to accompany Good to great : why some companies make the leap--and others don't (New York: Harpercollins, 2005).

Made in the USA
Middletown, DE
12 January 2018